The Biggest Mistakes in History

2008 to 2016

By

Robert Villegas

The Biggest Mistakes in History – 2008 to 2016

By

Robert Villegas

Published in the United States of America

Series Title: Villegas Politics Volume 2

Email **robertv1989@outlook.com**

Social Media Addresses

Blog: https://v4vendata.blogspot.com
CloutHub @RobertVillegas
MeWe www.mewe.com/i/robertvillegas
Minds @Robertv1989
Gab @V4Vendata
GETTR @V4Vendata
WIMKIN Robert Villegas
X: RobertVillegasJ

Dedicated to my friends

Steve and Paul

Table of Contents

Introduction

To be the Chief Executive of the greatest country in the world requires a leader with a great deal of knowledge, experience and reasoning ability. It requires having the very best minds as advisors, minds that the President can count on to give reasoned arguments and detailed knowledge about the important issues of the day. I think it takes a special ability to understand the principle of cause and effect concerning how government action impacts the lives of real people. Above all, it takes a keen understanding of history as well as deep insight into the philosophical principles that informed men during our years of founding. The President of the United States must be wise beyond his years even if he is an older man.

The question of how the President should handle the most pressing issues of the day is the province, not only of philosophers who wrote centuries ago, not only of the intellectuals and college professors who teach in our universities, but of the average citizen who must vote in an informed way. Our nation is run by its people.

This means that in the USA, the leader of the country is not the President but the informed citizen: YOU. It is your responsibility to tell your chosen agents in the government what they should do, the principles to which they should adhere and, especially, when the nation has gone in the wrong direction and how they can correct their course. Finally, you must expect your designated representatives to make decisions based upon the widest available knowledge and when they do not, when they have gone off course, you have to replace them with the right people.

For instance, the President must have available to him the widest range of scholarly and professional opinions on the key issues of the day. His advisors must be men of profound experience with the highest of intellects, men with access to the widest accumulated knowledge as well as the historical precedents that animate and give rise to an understanding of the issues. In order for the President to make a final decision, nothing must be left unexamined and all relevant factors must be taken into consideration. And, as you read about the ideas and actions of your leaders, you must be assured that they are objective and reasonable people.

I've often admired the ambiance of the White House. On the walls and throughout the building, you see ancient paintings and sculptures that remind us of the magnificent history of our country and the wisdom of many past Presidents. Each man is presented to us as someone who handled incredibly difficult questions and who possessed the knowledge and experience that made the country a better place. Men like Madison and Jefferson saw beyond the immediate political struggle and chose instead to advance enduring principles that applied to all men. Rather than preach re-distribution, they argued for liberty. Rather than promise prosperity in the here and now, they argued for liberty. Rather than promise programs to solve all invented "problems", they argued for liberty. They knew that liberty, leaving men free to solve their own problems, was the proper thing to do. Today, there are no descendants of our past Presidents.

Another important tool that a President needs is a firm grasp of history and the philosophical movements that have created it. This history must be based upon broad principles that are accurate and well-understood. For instance, if the President thinks that re-distribution will solve a particular problem, he should consult competent economists and historians who will tell him that the end does not justify the means and that, throughout history, re-distribution did not create any appreciable improvement. On the other hand, if the President adheres to Marxist premises that capitalism is evil then his policies will gravitate to arguments for the sacrifice of the affluent on behalf of the non-affluent. A good historian might point out the utter prejudice of that judgment and that history has not produced a system more affluent and fair than capitalism. He might even inform the President that capitalism, in essence, is about leaving all men free to solve their own problems and to live morally – and more importantly that capitalism requires the protection of individual rights and not their violation. An intelligent President would see the wisdom of these ideas.

One man honored at the White House, George Washington, struggled to build the nation in war and to preserve it as it strove to find its character. We are reminded of his famous advice to the nation that helped it prevail once his counsel was no longer available. I am privileged to have visited his home at Mount Vernon, enjoyed the beautiful countryside that he loved and stood upon the banks of the Potomac River. I saw the bed where he died and stood next to his casket. I wondered, on that beautiful day, what he would think of today's leaders. In Washington's hands, our nation was a reflection of the ideals and moral premises of the people who put him into the leadership of our nation. They saw in this great man the culmination of the spirit for life that made the people what they were; owners of the spirit of adventure and freedom.

Then there is Lincoln, who struggled with many crucial questions about the nature of the Union, the principles for which it stood and how to preserve those principles. The people elected him because they felt he reflected the love for freedom that belonged to all men of all colors and origins. They expected that he would reflect their values and their dedication to freedom. I wonder at the kind of dedication it must have taken for him as he stood on the balcony of the White House and looked out over the nation he led. I admire his vast wisdom and his certainty in the rightness of his course, a certainty that knew the meaning of the principle that "all men are created equal". I marvel at the brevity and universality of his Gettysburg Address.

One hopes for the wisdom of every holder of the Office of the Presidency. Our nation needs knowledgeable, experienced people who understand that the principles of this nation are universal, wise and seriously considered. A leader of this country must respect this wisdom that built our nation, understand the reasons behind its principles and honor those principles when he takes the oath of office.

Yet, the mistakes of the Obama Presidency were not made by an appeal to wisdom. They were made by men uncritically following a host of intellectuals and citizens who offered a different standard of moral worth. And, what's worse, the people who elected them did not do their job properly either. They made their decisions too lightly, perhaps were not well-informed and, even more importantly, thought that a little bit of re-distribution was fine. When the people are educated according to the ideas of collectivism, altruism and deception, then the country can get off course and the results not only corrupt men morally, they also impoverish the people.

In order to explain my meaning, I would like to embark on an analysis of some of the biggest mistakes in history. Through this book, I will show the importance of knowledge in the Presidency and how that knowledge can be used to solve some of our deepest problems. I'd like to show how the unwillingness to consider relevant knowledge can steer a nation off course and cause people to suffer. We will begin by analyzing some of President Obama's actions at the start of his Presidency.

Presidential Power

The first big mistake of the Obama administration was to assume that it was responsible for making every decision in the economy. This mistake was based upon the idea of an "activist" government that is responsible, not for protecting rights, but for creating rights and then taxing citizens who must pay for them. In practical terms, this view created a huge bottle neck for the entire country. Both large and small businesses, because they did not know how coming decisions would be made, began to curtail vital business decisions waiting for the administration to act.

To illustrate this mistake, and to learn the deeper causes of it, let's look at the idea of the Presidency that Mr. Obama held before he became our leader. In his speech on election night, he said:

"If there is anyone out there who still doubts that America is a place where all things are possible; who still wonders if the dream of our founders is alive in our time; who still questions the power of our democracy, tonight is your answer."[1]

The mistake here was to believe that the United States is a democracy. The trick here was a bait and switch; to say "democracy" when we are a republic which is a different concept. This deception creates tremendous problems for the nation.

You may think that I am quibbling but it is an important point and it gets to the heart of why the Obama

---

[1] Election Night Victory Speech

administration was a failure. Governance in a republic is a matter of playing by the rules established in a republic. This means honoring the Constitution and the protections it has put in place to secure liberty and safety for the people.

Our country is not a democracy – and to act as if it is, betrays a poor knowledge of history and of political philosophy. A democracy is a nation where the will of the majority rules. The classic example in Greece held that the majority could wield the power of life or death over any individual. As long as the majority voted upon it, anything could be done by the state. This leaves the door open to the gang that convinces people it speaks for them and gives it the incentive to rig votes and take dictatorial power.

When he took power, the President operated as a "ruler" rather than as a leader of a republic. He ignored the fact that our government operates according to a division of powers with checks and balances. Because he had talked about "democratic" principles during his campaign, he assumed that the election had given him a mandate to act unilaterally and ignore the Constitution. His basic argument: "We won."

This was a huge mistake, not only for the President, but also for the people who voted for him, especially those who thought they were voting for a man who would preserve and protect the Constitution.

The argument that a majority elected President Obama to do THEIR WILL was a false argument. In fact, the majority elected President Obama to preserve and protect the Constitution of the United States. It did not confer virtual dictatorial power upon him.

A constitutional scholar, as the President was reputed to be, should know this. The President can't just do whatever he wishes. There are principles embedded into the Constitution that protect against the abuse of Executive Power and it was the President's responsibility to do his job according to those principles. These are the principles of limited government which specify the rules under which the President can act. For instance, the President cannot act unilaterally. He can only enforce the laws passed by Congress. He cannot act alone and when he attempts to do so, Congress should stop him; the people should stop him.

What does the idea that we are a democracy lead to? Broken promises:

"America, this is our moment. This is our time. Our time to turn the page on the policies of the past. Our time to bring new energy and new ideas to the challenges we face. Our time to offer a new direction for the country we love.

"The journey will be difficult. The road will be long. I face this challenge with profound humility, and knowledge of my own limitations.

"But I also face it with limitless faith in the capacity of the American people. Because if we are willing to work for it, and fight for it, and believe in it, then I am absolutely certain that generations from now, we will be able to look back and tell our children that:
• This was the moment when we began to provide care for the sick and good jobs to the jobless; this was the moment when the rise of the oceans began to slow and our planet began to heal;
• This was the moment when we ended a war and secured our nation and restored our image as the last, best hope on Earth.
• This was the moment -- this was the time -- when we came together to remake this great nation so that it may always reflect our very best selves and our highest ideals."[2]

A government that promises these kinds of results sees itself as powerful enough to bring them about:

• It can virtually take over a large part of the economy and manage it (the automotive industry)
• It can engage in graft and "encourage" political contributions and payoffs (crony capitalism, GE, unions, Warren Buffett).
• It can pick winners and losers in the competitive economy, rewarding those who pay bribes and punishing those who don't (Solyndra and green energy subsidies).

---

[2] Primary Victory Speech

• It can create a dependent segment of voters who don't want to vote away their government-provided benefits (Health Care Legislation).
• It can be the arbiter of success and failure in the economy by creating regulations that favor friends and disfavor enemies (Dodd-Frank).
• It can eliminate any restrictions upon its activities by blatantly violating the Constitution and forcing hundreds of Constitutional challenges (British Petroleum, Executive Orders, Legislative Bribes in return for votes, etc., etc.).

Now we know why the President's first term was such a disaster and why the Tea Party took shape. "These are the times that try men's souls."

The Obama administration was making some of the biggest mistakes in history. This is because it was systematically operating as a de facto dictatorship, running roughshod over the Bill of Rights. I mentioned previously that the administration had taken the position, early on, that it was responsible for making all decisions in the economy. This was a serious over-reach even beyond the incredibly oppressive Bush policies of 2008. It was based upon an assumption made by President Obama that the election meant his views could override the Constitution. The consequence was that he established a mindset among his appointees that Executive action was more important than the separation of powers, that political outcomes were more important than individual rights.

The President was elected to lead and to enforce the laws of the land. He was not elected to create his own laws and blame the opposition for not cooperating with him. He was elected to work with the opposition and find common ground. He was not elected to verbally destroy his opposition and declare it unfit to make laws. He was elected to find a way within the confines of his designated powers. This also applied to his appointees.

"By the time he joined the Obama administration, Tim Geithner had settled on a narrative of the financial crisis that had the virtue of being nearly correct. As Geithner saw it, the government had faced two imperatives during that tumultuous time. The first was to stop the panic and save the banks. The second was to satisfy the country's bloodlust toward Wall Street. Geithner believed —and this was his real insight—that you could do only one or the other. Anything truly vengeful, such as cleaning out whole floors of executives or other forms of what Geithner called "Old Testament justice," could destroy the institutions you were trying to save. But anything merely symbolic—a firing here, and a perp walk there—the public would dismiss as a stunt."[3]

"And yet, when Geithner traveled a few hundred yards from his office to the White House for the daily senior staff meeting...he was surrounded, as it were, by petulance. The president's top aides were desperate to

[3] The Escape Artists: How the Obama Team Fumbled the Recover by Noam Scheiber Page 115, ebook version

solve the crisis. They were just as desperate to position the administration as resolutely anti-fat cat. They pleaded with Geithner to fire a bailed-out CEO. They begged him to hack away at executive pay."[4]

In these two paragraphs, author Noam Scheiber has inadvertently exposed the erroneous view that the government can properly do such things as fire executives and meddle with salaries. These people, the "aides" of our nation, appointed by the President, thought they could do virtually anything they wanted. They acted like bullies drunk with power, completely ignorant of the "rule of law". They acted as if they *were* the law. The proper question, then, was "Who did they think they were?"

I would like to remind you that during previous periods of our history, many American Presidents had a deep respect for the Constitution and the rule of law. There were times when an American President would never consider violating the rights of American citizens for the sake of a political goal. Doing such a thing was considered uncivilized and immoral. They knew that one of the cornerstones of a civilized society was respect for individual rights. During the Obama administration, such violations were done with impunity, as if they were normal. The President's aides were barbarians who didn't know it.

---

[4] Ibid

Contrary to the opinions of the President's aides, our country, when it was founded, was not intended to be a dictatorship. No one in government had the right or the authority to fire executives in the private sector. No one, except a judge (or police officer), had the authority to arrest any individual. First, there must be probable cause that a law (passed by Congress) had been violated; then there must be an arrest, a charge, a trial in a court of law and evidence. This does not come from the Treasury department but from the Justice Department that is also required to implement due process.

Timothy Geithner could fire CEOs. He had no authority to do that. Neither did the government have the authority to deal with issues of executive pay. Those issues are handled by private contracts. Certainly, the government proclaimed that these companies had accepted government bailout money and that the bailout was a de facto government takeover. But this line of reasoning only points out the ludicrous nature of the bailouts and what kind of things can happen when government oversteps its proper role.

Certainly, one could say that this dictatorship started under Bush and that Obama had nothing to do with it. I would remind people that by the time the bailouts were being considered by Congress, Obama had known that the election was swinging his way and he supported the bailouts, even participated in meetings about them as a candidate. So, it cannot be said that Obama did not have a significant role to play in the bailouts.

The government's presumption that it had the right to intervene in the economy was one of the grossest violations of individual rights in the history of the nation; and it was justified, as are all usurpations of power, by a ginned up emergency that supposedly threatened the entire fabric of our society.

The truth is that government actions taken by both Bush and Obama have prolonged the economic consequences of the housing crisis. As of today, almost eight years later, our economy still hangs on a thread. Had we allowed those companies to fail, we would be farther along toward a recovery (if not fully recovered by now). The government's actions served the purpose of re-distributing the problem to all parties in the economy, even those who would not have been harmed by the collapse. The money taken out of the economy for the bailout has also prolonged high levels of unemployment.

Had advisors in the Bush administration (and later in the Obama administration) refused to interfere in the dealings of private companies, these companies could have solved the issues of "insolvency" by normal private means; and this would have contained the damage. Certainly, it would have meant hard times for some people but those who were not party to the housing crisis would not have been harmed. Housing prices would have found their bottom and then recovered. Those who held toxic assets would have held on to them or sold them at a loss; companies dependent upon the success of the failed banks and institutions would have found other places for their investment dollars. The rights of all citizens to make their own economic decisions would have been preserved and the American economy would have quickly recovered.

But worse than the housing collapse and its effect on banking was the continuation of the re-distributive philosophy of the Obama administration. In order to deal with the collapse caused by re-distribution (due to the CRA), these very unwise men doubled down on re-distribution. They ignored Fannie and Freddie by allowing it to continue its policies. Then they re-distributed the American taxpayer's money to the failed banks that had been destroyed by Fannie and Freddie. Then, through huge stimulus programs, they redistributed more money to green energy debacles and leftist giveaways such as in the Pigford scandal. They blocked banks from foreclosing on unpaid loans and they insisted that those banks re-finance loans to people who could not make payments on them. To deal with the consequence of their policies on unemployment they increased unemployment and food stamp payments. To further "stimulate" the economy, they re-distributed more money to their favorites in leftist organizations that were already wasting billions of dollars. The examples of re-distribution were endless.

Finally, the government's policy toward "fat-cats" was nothing more than show designed to divert attention from the fiasco that the government had caused. It was not the fat-cats on Wall Street who caused the collapse; it was government bureaucrats at Fannie Mae and Freddie

Mac who had been issuing loans under the auspices of the Community Reinvestment Act. This is the real scandal that even a person as "intelligent" a Timothy Geithner ignored because the President wanted to exploit the emergency in order to increase the levels of re-distribution in the economy.

The financial crisis, created by people whose philosophy of re-distribution matched that of the President, was the pretext for the government taking over the banking industry. If you thought these jokers could save the banking industry, you were mistaken. They were the destroyers of it and their method of destruction was the same that caused the crisis: re-distribution.

The assumption of dictatorial power by the government during this crisis was what caused it to deepen and spread to the rest of the economy. The use of enormous amounts of taxpayer dollars was a theft of money held by individuals in private accounts and this theft was what contributed to our present problems.

"Government cannot make man richer, but it can make him poorer." - Ludwig von Mises

Understanding the President
Since he came onto the political scene, everyone has been trying to figure out what motivated President Obama; what made him tick?

Some people point to his community organizing days when he learned to shakedown businesses through a "protester for hire" scheme that benefited paying customers. Others point to the sundry socialists and communists that populated his childhood and college years. Others point to his large ego or his "thin skin". Others point to his tendency to govern through Executive Orders or Presidential decrees which reflects a disdain for views that he considers to be completely wrong. Others think he was abused as a child or that he was a closet communist consciously seeking the destruction of our nation on behalf of a foreign power.

You'll find articles on the Internet where semi-competent psychologists and doctors tried to understand what was wrong with the President. Why was he so aloof and detached from real people? All of these analyses missed the point.

If you want to figure out this President you have to look for the one key principle that guided his every action. And on this count, he was finally transparent. You will find this principle behind every thought, every act, every bill, every speech, every utterance, every corruption and every suggestion he made on how you can live a better life. The principle was altruism. Barack Obama was a committed altruist and his every policy advanced the principle of self-sacrifice.

I think our President, unlike every President before him, with the possible exception of Jimmy Carter, has essentially two psychological attachments that make up his core philosophical premises: 1) altruism and 2) a false belief that altruism actually makes things better. He will always believe the first and his Presidency was spent grappling with the failure of the second.

You might recall the famous dialogue between candidate Obama and "Joe the Plumber" when he informed the electorate of his opinion that re-distributing money to some people was better for everyone. This statement elicited the ire of many people who saw the President's view as a form of Marxism where the government violates the rights of productive people, turns them into virtual slaves and enriches those who are not self-sufficient or productive. Many saw this view as the direct opposite of the principles upon which our nation was founded, principles such as property rights, individual responsibility, voluntary trade and keeping the results of your work. Indeed, many people saw it as an expression of the Marxist principle "from each according to his ability to each according to his need". In fact, this was true and it exposes the fact that Marx's maxim was an expression of altruism. Marxism was all about altruistic re-distribution in exactly the same way meant in the President's comments to Joe the Plumber.

In making that statement to Joe, Obama expressed his belief that people have a duty to work for the sake of others rather than themselves. With altruism, sacrifice is the hallmark of the moral life and anyone who lives for himself is considered to be a selfish brute who deserves ostracism and expropriation.

I think our President, almost instinctively, used altruism during his presidency as a way to obtain and maintain power, as if altruism was a magic formula with which no one could disagree. And about this, he was thoroughly convinced. He even cultivated a mystique, a personality cult where you can almost see a magical aura around him, a saintly quality that ritually motivates people to work toward collective goals. In other words, his basic motivation has always been to encourage in every American the exact opposite of the pursuit of happiness. The President was at war with happiness. That few people realized this was why so many couldn't figure him out.

Was the President aware of the cronyism that his policies made possible, the Al Capone aspect of many things he did? I think so. Like Saul Alinsky, who was a strong influence on him, his methods were not only replete with agitation, but also union-friendly. Additionally, it was said that he sometimes sent his trained protestors out to harass and embarrass the competitors of some of his community partners. As was clear, Democratic policies in Chicago were not immune from the pay-off and the quid-pro-quo. And, as was typical with such "gangsterism", the ready defense was the idea that the end (helping the poor) justifies the means. There was no reason why the "middle man", the community organizer, could not also embellish his own life.

A good example was the rampant cronyism of his energy policies. He considered that it was good to harm the interests of the fossil fuel industry because of the supposed damage they were doing to the economy, there was nothing wrong with regulating them out of existence and giving tax payer dollars to the chosen few among his friends who were offering alternative options. That much of this money was wasted and or stolen did not bother the President at all in view of the "good" that his energy policy was trying to accomplish.[5]

For the President, the end, the sacrifice of every productive person in the country, justifies the means, lies, treachery and deceit. Everything he did in the name of altruism was another way to launder money to leftists, re-distribute it to his supporters while also extorting it from productive businesspeople through propagandized emergencies that he and his friends in the media created. His basic method of operation was to excoriate private companies for not caring about people and taking the payoff on the down low.

Our President had a fixation on altruism. When speaking to college students, he told them to go into public service rather than private business. When dealing with executives he assumed it was their duty to give in to his "superior" but non-existent wisdom. In taking over the auto companies, he criticized investors in Chrysler for not

---

[5] For an excellent antidote to the Presidents energy policies, read "The Moral Case for Fossil Fuels" by Alex Epstein.

sharing in the sacrifice. When addressing the subprime crisis, he demanded that taxpayers and banks pay to keep people in their homes. When taking over college loans he cavalierly assumed that taxpayers should put up the money for college education while counselling students to do community service in return. He put millions of productive people out of work in order to pay for the Stimulus Package that created no jobs for those very same people. And he repeatedly packed his bills with millions of dollars in pork that benefited leftist charity organizations. At every step of the way, he offered up sacrifice as the only solution for every problem - and today all of these problems are worse than when he started. They didn't work.

The President did not understand what it meant to pursue happiness because his entire life had been based on exhorting people to sacrifice. He did not know that the pursuit of happiness was a far superior motivation than the call to give up one's product. His enemy was the principle that makes possible cooperation, self-interest, the rule of law and capital accumulation. He warred against the principle of civilized living while exuding the aura of a civilized man.

Nor did he realize that the perennial call to sacrifice was not a principle that worked; it was the lowest principle of all, a destructive and uncivilized idea, the justification used by dictators and potentates for theft, plunder, robbery and violation of honest people.

What made President Obama the worst President in our history was his advocacy of sacrifice as a high ideal. Contrary to his own view, his was not a morality derived from the height of intelligence, the culmination of the best education, the greatest principle ever to be learned; an idea so true that only someone truly evil and selfish would disagree. It does not take high intelligence to conclude that harming some people to benefit others is counterproductive. Most hard working people have figured out that their own lives are diminished when others are encouraged to take the dole and not to work.

Indeed, you must ask yourself, how difficult did this advocacy of sacrifice make his job as President? When the only guide a President has is the belief that "Selfishness is always the problem and sacrifice is always the solution", how aloof and detached would such a President need to be? Imagine *that* slogan on the President's desk replacing Truman's maxim "The Buck Stops Here". For President Obama, the buck stops at the hard working tax payer. Yet, if sacrifice were truly the singular magic formula for Presidential problem solving, anyone could be President. Even Barack Obama. No proof required, no logic needed, just this simple non sequitur as a way of life. "When someone hurts, find someone to hurt." Eight years of that and a Noble Peace prize to boot.

The Kansas Speech
"I am not one of those whom one may ask about their why" – Nietzsche (Thus Spake Zarathustra)

Whenever a nation faces great challenges, the leader of that nation must tell the truth. He must stand upon a lectern so high that the entire nation can hear and ponder his important words. He must carefully explain the situation, how the nation got there and what must be done to correct the mistakes of the past. To use a cliché, only the whole truth can help a people muster the courage necessary to save the nation. Only the whole truth can clear minds and establish the proper agenda for victory.

For a true leader, this is not a problem. Truth and honesty are part of his life. He became successful by correctly assessing a number of situations and he has proven his leadership under fire, among real people or on the battlefield. He also knows that he cannot solve human problems by lying to the people. He must be sufficiently analytical and self-critical, so much so that he is able to discover the flaw, even in his own philosophy, that has caused the nation's problems; and he is forthcoming about that flaw. Times of crisis are not times for rationalization, excuse making and narcissism. If a leader thinks he can rationalize his own failings, then the nation will not be well-served.

But the truth requires more than just a statement of fact. The correct context must be established and the leader must understand that the unseen is often the cause of the seen. He must grasp the fact that it is his responsibility to be dispassionate, even self-critical, if he is to earn trust. Such a person must have a commitment to the truth and he must express it clearly and with dignity. He is the embodiment of the people's struggle, the repository of their hope and the representative of their aspirations for a better life. He must know that he holds the survival of the nation in his hands and that the lives of people are at stake. Only a great leader can clarify the moral issues upon which a nation is founded and only a great leader can muster the honesty necessary to point out the moral principles upon which survival will be based.

Our nation is on the precipice of disaster. Millions of individuals are without jobs, many of them have lost their homes and many live in homes worth less than the amount owed on them. The cost of transportation is going up. The cost of food is going up and there is no end in sight to the suffering. Society will collapse if the negative trends continue. Government policies have caused these sufferings and only a change in government policy will rectify them.

In the midst of this suffering, President Obama gave a speech in Kansas in December of 2011, in the virtual center of the country. In this speech, he spelled out what he considers to be the truth; how he thinks we got to this position, the principles we have disregarded and the solution to our problems. He wanted the nation to rally around him and accept his philosophy as our best hope. He also wanted us to reelect him so he could do more of what he had been doing to "solve" our problems.

As I will show, the speech was full of lies and any rational person could see that this man was not up to the task of leadership. The speech was full of so many rationalizations, so many fallacies, so many excuses and false solutions that any clear thinking individual could have seen that this man did not deserve re-election.

Yet, the aftermath of the speech exposed the fact that our situation was worse than we had thought. It exposed a leadership vacuum, not only with the President, but with his opposition as well. There appeared to be no one who could answer the President; there was no one capable of telling the truth; no one who could rise to the occasion; no one who could tell us why we were bankrupt monetarily and morally. The President's speech may have given us lies, but the opposition to him was silent.

Why was that? I think it was because the opposition to the President could not refute what the President said in his speech. The opposition was swimming in the same river, so to speak. Republican politicians agree with every major premise the President accepted and because there really was no opposition, there was no one in the public arena who could save the nation. Where were Gingrich and Romney on this speech? Why didn't they speak up? Where was the response that will answer the President in clear, believable terms? Certainly, in the midst of all this nihilism, no one could clearly articulate the flaws in the President's economic policy. Where was the opposition leader up to the challenge of history?

So, if none of our leaders will provide the truth about the President's speech in Kansas, someone else will have to do it.

At the beginning of his speech the President built up his first key concept: optimism.

"My grandparents served during World War II. He was a soldier in Patton's army; she was a worker on a bomber assembly line. And together, they shared the optimism of a nation that triumphed over the Great Depression and over fascism. They believed in an America where hard work paid off, and responsibility was rewarded, and anyone could make it if they tried – no matter who you were, no matter where you came from, no matter how you started out.

"And these values gave rise to the largest middle class and the strongest economy that the world has ever known. It was here in America that the most productive workers, the most innovative companies turned out the best products on Earth. And you know what? Every American shared in that pride and in that success – from those in the executive suites to those in middle management to those on the factory floor. So you could have some confidence that if you gave it your all, you'd take enough home to raise your family and send your kids to school and have your health care covered, put a little away for retirement."

One thing that characterized most of the President's speeches, and I've noticed it since his first "important" speech in 2004, was that he thought in non-essentials. What this meant was that the principles that underlie his statements were not based on fundamentals but quite often on derivatives of fundamentals. To elaborate; was "optimism" really what made depression-era Americans successful? Or was optimism merely a characteristic derived from a more fundamental characteristic such as the fact that they possessed the uncompromising characteristics of a free people? This means that optimism was really an outgrowth of freedom and, since this was true, it was better to derive the attitudes of the World War 2 generation from freedom rather than from a derivative of freedom.

You might ask why was this question important? How did it impact the values the President was trying to explicate? First of all, a lack of conceptual clarity, thinking in non-essentials, influences decisions and proposed solutions. If the President was going to talk about what made Americans succeed during that period when his grandparents lived, shouldn't he have referred to their basic characteristics rather than non-essential or derivative characteristics? Secondly, it was important to ensure that we weren't being manipulated in some way. Thinking in non-essentials is a characteristic of leaders who don't understand where they are and where they are going. In other words, they may be leading you down the wrong road for the sake of their own agendas rather than yours. Or their thinking may be so muddled that their pronouncements hit a wrong chord, so to speak. They don't ring true and lead in the wrong direction.

This is the problem of thinking in non-essentials: you develop an inability to know, in terms of essentials, what you should do. For instance, if you accept "optimism" as a key characteristic of past Americans you cannot then decide which type of government people should establish. Optimism, not being a fundamental principle, does not explain how man survives. It does not explain how people determine their core values, their core philosophies, their needs, desires and ideas. With optimism as your guide, you cannot identify which essential measures the government should take in order to secure the safety and rights of individuals. The term is without content, standards and meaning.

Optimism is not the key characteristic that made our grandparents' generation successful. This generation suffered greatly and they were poorly served by their political leadership. Most were not highly educated and they certainly did not have a sense of optimism about the future. In fact, they had been beaten down by poverty and unemployment, hunger and homelessness. Those not completely destroyed by it, learned how to survive; they became rugged, practical and dedicated to the survival of their families. What they did have was the ability to survive and the determination to overcome incredible obstacles. This was a legacy, fundamentally, of the freedom they possessed and the ethical standards made possible by that freedom. Yes, they were strong, resilient and committed to their families; but they were also free during a period of history when the world was moving toward collectivism. They saw this trend and decided they wanted no part of it. **They did not want to live as slaves.** And that was the fundamental reason they fought and won the war.

Certainly, one could say, in a sense, that they were optimistic about the future, and they had many of the traits of their ancestors and they certainly hoped for a better day. But the method of thinking in non-essentials served to smuggle in the real principle that the President wanted us to accept uncritically. That he assigned optimism to a status of fundamental smuggled in his belief that optimism was a collective trait infused with collective human qualities such as the willingness to sacrifice and work hard for the sake of others; in other words, to support the goals of the collectivists in society.

The implication of the President's statement, and this gets to the thinking method that was so obvious in his speeches, was that any characteristic that is collective in nature, or derived from collective traits, is fundamental. This is an aspect of the "straw man" fallacy that he often displayed. If you disagreed about what he considered to be fundamental, in this case the straw man of collective optimism, anyone who was against optimism must necessarily be against collectivism and its "positive" aspects. They must, of necessity, be anti-man. Notice, this precluded (or edged out) a consideration of other possible causes of our nation's greatness. He put you in a position in which thinking that man was not optimistic, necessarily made you his opponent and a capitalist.

The President, and many others, would have you believe that it was because Americans were collectively minded, that they sacrificed for others and fought to save their communities – that this was the goal Americans fought for in World War 2: stronger communities. Again, wanting stronger communities was a non-essential that the President had assumed to be essential.

And again, here's the problem of thinking in non-essentials: if the President wanted to be genuine, truly lead and inspire, he would identify the real fundamental principles that our forefathers held, not some Dale Carnegie course approximations. If the President wanted to inspire people, he would have dealt in universal principles that ring true. The idea that "optimism" was what gave people the courage to win a war is false. Can you imagine a soldier heading into battle, with mortar shells going off all around him, saying to his buddy: "I'm going to kill those Germans because I'm optimistic about the future and I want to have stronger communities back home."?

Our grandparents succeeded because they were free thinkers, individualists, who refused to live as slaves. Individualism has many consequences. For instance, an individualist has the ability to think and speak as he deems fit. He can act and be goal-oriented. He has the freedom and the desire to succeed. Individualism releases a person to "be himself" so to speak and, in another respect, to create his own character and live a moral life. The individualist has a strong desire to be self-reliant and to keep the results of his work. In fact, the individualist does not like to be ruled, preached to, commanded or directed. The American individualist will fight when you threaten his freedom; and he will join others in that fight. But he is not, fundamentally fighting *for* those others. He is cooperating with them to win the war. And this is what helped Americans defeat the depression and the war. To the President, individualism was "famous" but not fundamental.

But individualism was not the idea toward which the President was aiming. His goal was not to release you to defeat an enemy but to ensure that you voted for him; and toward this goal, he preferred that you have "optimism", collective pride and a willingness to sacrifice. He preferred that you think in non-essentials because that was his only hope of keeping his job when he made that speech in Kansas.

In his speech, the President said:

"Today, we're still home to the world's most productive workers. We're still home to the world's most innovative companies. But for most Americans, the basic bargain that made this country great has eroded. Long before the recession hit, hard work stopped paying off for too many people. Fewer and fewer of the folks who contributed to the success of our economy actually benefited from that success. Those at the very top grew wealthier from their incomes and their investments – wealthier than ever before. But everybody else struggled with costs that were growing and paychecks that weren't – and too many families found themselves racking up more and more debt just to keep up."

Here the President was attempting to provide a reason why the "optimism" of the previous statement had been "eroded". Yes, the President said, we still had the most productive workers and the most innovative companies, but the "basic bargain" had been eroded, hard work stopped paying off for too many people. What does this mean? Who eroded the "basic bargain"? What was that basic bargain? How was it brought about? Who made it possible?

The basic bargain to which the President referred was a sort of implicit contract that if you "give it your all" you have some assurance that you'll be able to take care of your family, have your health care taken care of and put away money for retirement. It was this "bargain" that had been eroded, according to the President. The "middle class" was no longer receiving the benefit of the "basic bargain" and someone was responsible for that: "those at the top".

Before we go back to the President's speech, we must establish the full context. First of all, we should understand what made possible those "most productive workers" and "most innovative companies" to which the

President referred because this understanding will give you a clue to just who was being exploited in our society at the time of the speech. I think it is important to have this background if we are to think in essentials. Indeed, you can't decide what to do in the future if you don't know the essential principles that got us where we are.

How does a nation accomplish productive workers and innovative companies? Not every nation has been able to do this and it is important to be clear about the ideas and values that create prosperity. In other words, what must we have in the way of economic principles in order to build a vibrant economy and even come up with a "basic bargain"?

History has provided an answer: capitalism. Capitalism is *the* prerequisite of prosperity. Remove capitalism from a nation and you have no prosperity. Why is this? What is so good about capitalism that it creates such productive workers and innovative products?

Productive workers don't grow on trees. They don't just have optimism and want to work hard. There is a reason for their optimism and hard work. As Ayn Rand has pointed out: "Capitalism is the system that made productive cooperation possible among men, on a large scale—a voluntary cooperation that raised everyone's standard of living—as the nineteenth century has demonstrated."[6]

---

[6] How To Read (And Not To Write), The Ayn Rand Letter Vol. 1, No. 26 September 25, 1972

The fact that capitalism enables voluntary cooperation was missed by the President and his economic advisers. And they had no idea why voluntary cooperation was accomplished more effectively by capitalism rather than by collectivism (that requires cooperation through shared sacrifice). Capitalism is inferior in their minds because it is only about "playing by your own rules" and stealing from people. This view sees exploiters everywhere and it misses the spectacle of millions of individual acts of mutually beneficial cooperation that take place every day under capitalism.

Rand also provides the definition of capitalism:

"Capitalism is a social system based on the recognition of individual rights, including property rights, in which all property is privately owned.

"The recognition of individual rights entails the banishment of physical force from human relationships: basically, rights can be violated only by means of force. In a capitalist society, no man or group may initiate the use of physical force against others. The only function of the government, in such a society, is the task of protecting man's rights, i.e.., the task of protecting him from physical force; the government acts as the agent of man's right of self-defense, and may use force only in retaliation and only against those who initiate its use; thus the government is the means of placing the retaliatory use of force under objective control."[7]

Now that is thinking in essentials. It clearly lays the foundation for why our system, our once capitalist system, was so successful.

Yet, according to Obama progressives, capitalism was not about the banishment of physical force; but about the use of physical force through government to create monopolies, get special privileges and steal from the consumers who have no choice but to work in the factories and use the products. They ignore the men who rose from poverty to become some of the most successful industrialists in the world; whose enterprises provided virtually all of the luxuries we enjoy today. They ignore the elevating standards of living, the longer life-spans, the mobility and self-confidence that people enjoyed because they held their destinies in their own hands. They ignore the millions of morally proper decisions that people make daily even in our own compromised semi-capitalist system. They ignore the fact that capitalist systems tend to be more peaceful and secure because people who earn their own livings do not feel compelled to violate the property rights of others and they want to enjoy their lives rather than sacrifice them in endless and unnecessary wars.

---

[7] What is Capitalism, Capitalism: the Unknown Ideal by Ayn Rand

Leftists cannot think in terms of essentials. If they were to do such a distasteful thing, they would not be leftists. Essentially, they don't understand that survival is about work and that any system that liberates man to pursue survival through production and trade is one that creates millions of mutually beneficial trades every day. They confuse production with force and criticize production as if it means a zero-sum transaction where one person wins and gets rich and the other person loses and becomes poor. They ignore the fact that it is capitalism, and nothing else, that created the middle class. So they proclaim themselves champions of the middle class while they seek to destroy or undermine the source of voluntary cooperation: capitalism. And they countenance physical force by government, the very idea that capitalism prohibits, in order to rectify what they consider to be problems created by capitalism (that they, the leftists, created through their own coercive policies).

Progressives act as if they are righteous defenders of the average man, protectors of the rights of man, as if they were fighting dictators not industrialists. They posture as courageous critics of a corrupt system while ignoring the fact that the capitalist "dictators" they denigrate are merely clear thinking men who have mastered the art of production, not the art of conquest. They don't understand what it takes to create and manage a thriving corporation because they have never done it and they let their altruist morality cloud their minds to the fact that capitalism has lifted more people out of poverty than any of the sundry dictators they admire. Where capitalism enables thriving, socialism enables murder; and yet they don't see it – they don't see the killing fields and mass graves.

They also don't see the beautiful cities of capitalism, the tall buildings, the bustling factories and the brilliant shops offering stunning products. They don't see the automobiles and the jet airplanes and the HDTVs, the 5-speaker sound systems and the iPods and iPhones. Instead, they imagine dead bodies and starving children in the clutches of a blood thirsty capitalist eager for plunder. They proclaim that capitalism would just as soon let people starve for the sake of profit without noticing that the real starving people in the world are those trapped by the progressives' view of the world.

And what is their view of the world? Like all altruists, they believe man is evil at base and incapable of being moral. They send out this teaching through every pronouncement and judgment that they can. They treat individuals, especially the productive and rich ones, as expendable and particularly worthy of ridicule. Since their morality holds that man should sacrifice for others, they see man's inability to be totally self-sacrificial as a black mark on man. Therefore, the most successful, those who practice sacrifice the least, are viewed as particularly evil and deserving of forced sacrifice, control and punishment. If you notice a similarity between this view and the views of some of the most brutal tribal leaders of the past including some of the most monstrous dictators, the similarity is not a coincidence.

What is the greatest threat to capitalism, peace and cooperation? It is the progressives' view of man coupled with the idea of collectivism, the modern form of primitive tribal organization; the idea that people must cluster into bands or tribes and battle one another for political power. Anti-capitalism is essentially anti-reason and anti-man in the same way that collectivism is anti-individual. It is a desire to destroy the good because the good is unwilling to grovel at the altar of self-sacrifice.

Don't proclaim that altruists really want to do good things for people. There are two sides to the altruism coin. One side is protestations of love for man while the other side is protestations of hatred for everything. One side, the side of professed love, is the outward expression of altruism that keeps altruists in the game of acting on their hatred. And this brings us back to the President's speech.

The President, by proclaiming a love and support of the middle class, declared that the enemy of the middle class was the very system that created the middle class: capitalism.

Yet, capitalism can only exist in a nation where the government protects individual rights and the rule of law. Its basic principle is that the individual is free to use his own mind, create his own survival and keep the results of his work. It declares that man is essentially good, capable of reason and that he acquires his survival through production and trade with others, by means of reason. What does capitalism require? Capitalism requires freedom, freedom to think, freedom to evaluate reality, to make judgments, to develop products, to obtain capital, to trade and to keep the results of one's work. The President will have none of that.

Remember what I said about the character of the American people in the pre-war and wartime period; that their victories were made possible by the fact that they were free. Their freedom meant they were free to live, to think, to invest and to create...they were not regulated into prosperity; their Constitution liberated them to create that prosperity because the Founders knew that their hard work and thought would directly benefit them and that a government that protected their rights is the most advanced government possible.

Because of capitalism, the American spirit was free to win the war and this spirit, this sense of life, released upon the world a "can do" attitude that says anything is possible if you are free to act. Capitalism means freedom to survive; not just for "those at the top" but for all Americans. Americans become "those at the top" (compared to the rest of the world) by producing and investing their own savings (for retirement). The middle class was created when Americans were liberated to work in the factories; liberated to become the workers, middle managers and the upper managers. Without capitalism you do not have productive workers, upward mobility, innovative companies or a middle class. Without capitalism, you cannot win a global war or stamp out poverty or defend the middle class.

How could the President have been a defender of the middle class when he did not seem to understand this critical point about freedom - and especially about capitalism? How could he, on the one hand, champion optimism and on the other hand champion re-distribution of the income of optimistic and free individuals? Did he not know that re-distribution destroys the freedom and optimism of the productive? Wasn't he turning the producers into slaves through re-distribution? How could he, on the one hand, claim to be liberating producers, "those at the top", while on the other hand raising taxes upon them? How could he, on the one hand, praise the free market, while on the other hand create oppressive regulations that stifled economic activity? How could he, on the one hand, recognize that Americans are productive and our factories innovative while on the other hand not even acknowledging that it was capitalism that brought it about? And if it was capitalism that brought this situation about, how could he, on any hand, claim that "playing by your own rules" was what brought capitalism down and ended the "basic bargain" when it was capitalism that enabled them to play by their own rules and create prosperity?

So the real question should have been not how did we lose our optimism and the "basic bargain". The real questions should have been "how did we lose capitalism?" and "how can we get it back?" And the real answer should be, by eliminating regulations, letting people play by their own rules and return to the Bill of Rights.

In his speech, the President said:

"Now, for many years, credit cards and home equity loans papered over this harsh reality. But in 2008, the house of cards collapsed. We all know the story by now: mortgages sold to people who couldn't afford them, or even sometimes understand them. Banks and investors allowed to keep packaging the risk and selling it off. Huge bets – and huge bonuses – made with other people's money on the line. Regulators who were supposed to warn us about the dangers of all this, but looked the other way or didn't have the authority to look at all.

"It was wrong. It combined the breathtaking greed of a few with irresponsibility all across the system. And it plunged our economy and the world into a crisis from which we're still fighting to recover. It claimed the jobs and the homes and the basic security of millions of people – innocent, hardworking Americans who had met their responsibilities but were still left holding the bag."

The implication here was that the house of cards collapsed because of...wait for it...irresponsible greed, meaning unregulated capitalism. It was because people wanted to make money that the house collapsed, and, the President thinks, it was wrong. But let's look a little deeper. The President talks about the fact that mortgages were sold to people who couldn't afford them. Who was responsible for that? Issuing these bad mortgages was caused by a regulatory scheme that was set up to re-distribute bank loans from credit-worthy borrowers to non-credit-worthy borrowers. Certainly, these bad mortgages would not have been given by a rational bank manager seeking to make money; he would have known that the loans were questionable and that issuing so many of them could potentially destroy his bank. Why did "rational" bank managers seeking to make money issue so many bad loans? Was it really greed for big bonuses that was responsible for the subprime fiasco? Dig deeper and you find that this was done because of *government* regulations that forced banks to issue and solicit these bad loans. And, you will also find that President Obama approved of this issuance of bad loans.

Which group of people created and favored these programs? The answer is progressives of the "New Deal" variety. In fact, the Community Reinvestment Act (CRA), which was passed in the '70s, was strengthened in 1994 after a law suit that claimed banks were guilty of racial discrimination when deciding who got home loans. The goal of these lawsuits was to force the banks to issue more loans to poor people. The strengthened CRA, favored by Democrats, demanded that banks prove they were not discriminating against blacks under threat of prosecution by the Clinton Justice Department. And it was a willing and enthusiastic supporter of President Obama, namely ACORN[8], that encouraged poor people to take these loans. They even had a working scheme in place to take advantage of the CRA regulations; they advertised to poor people that they should come into ACORN to be

---

[8] Association of Community Organizations for Reform Now

helped in applying for these loans. In addition, Fannie Mae and Freddie Mac bought these loans and "bundled" them into investment packages to be sold to financial institutions as top-rated securities. Certainly, there was some fraud involved here. The people at Fannie and Freddie who got those huge bonuses that the President complained about were Democratic bundlers and friends of Democrats.

The strengthening of the CRA which put banks on notice that they needed to issue more loans to the poor was a failed re-distribution scheme fostered by progressives. This scheme caused the stock market to collapse, TARP to be created and the literal theft of almost one half of the savings of many middle class Americans. Yet, not one government official has been charged with a crime. It was the government, not capitalism, that was responsible for the collapse and it was progressives, including President Obama, who lobbied and sued the government to create this entire scheme. So now, one of the architects of the fiasco (the President), tells us that it was not caused by the people who forced the banks to issue the mortgages (the Clinton administration), or the people who shook down the banks (ACORN), or the Democrats who forced banks to prove they weren't racist (Dodd and Frank) and solicited (pressured) poor people to apply for the loans (again ACORN). In spite of this, we are supposed to believe that the real problem was "greed". Was the President fingering his own greed or that of his employer ACORN? I don't think so. He was complaining about unregulated capitalism against which he and his friends wrote the regulations.

Understand what I am saying: all of these bad decisions that the President criticizes in his Kansas speech were decisions made by people who share the President's philosophy of re-distribution and they were undertaken by institutions created to effect that re-distribution. These include Fannie Mae, Freddie Mac, government appointed heads of those companies, Countrywide, supporter of Democratic politicians, a Democratic Congress, Barney Frank, Chris Dodd, and an organization trained by Obama named ACORN; all of whom claimed to be working on behalf of the "poor". Yet, this all sounds like altruism to me, not greed. So what was the President talking about? Where was his honesty about his role in creating this fiasco? And where were Dodd and Frank? They were writing more regulations to control financial institutions in order to paper-over their own corruption. They were blaming the whole fiasco on the banks when they should have blamed it on themselves.

Why wasn't the altruism inherent in these programs blamed for the economic collapse? It was not greed but socialist principles that sacrificed the savings of the middle class in order to give homes to the lower class. It wasn't unfettered capitalism that had failed but unfettered socialism. The actors whose philosophy caused the collapse were involved in socialist irresponsibility, not capitalism. Why didn't the media pick up on this?

The answer was pretty simple: socialism doesn't work and they were invested in socialism. The cold, hard truth is that socialism is the means through which a smart criminal can cover up the fact that he is stealing money. All he has to do is say he is doing it for the poor. And rather than expose the charlatan scam that caused the financial collapse of the most powerful economy in history, the media looked the other way. And they allowed the President to blame the fiasco on an institution, capitalism, that was raped and violated by the scam.

It should be no surprise that one of the lawyers involved in changing the CRA back in 1994, President Obama, was the one person who benefited most from the economic collapse. Not only was he able to skim some of the stolen money for his Presidential campaigns (he was one of the largest recipients of Fannie and Freddie campaign contributions), but when the economy collapsed, it paved the way for his election as President. Although he and his progressive friends caused the collapse, the Republicans got blamed. In fact, Obama would probably have lost the election were it not for the collapse made possible by the failed policies he advocated. Was it a coincidence or a plot? I'll let you decide.

Needless to say, the President wouldn't blame himself for the financial collapse, nor did he want to blame his own philosophy. But his denials didn't change the truth. And this was a time when honesty and truth were required (as if there is ever a time when they are not). Rather than tell you the brutal honest truth, the President would rather play politics and continue to assert in a major economic speech that capitalism (not playing by the rules) was the cause of the problems that he had helped to create.

The truth is that the philosophy destroying our economy then and now is altruism, the philosophy of the President. Did he care that re-distributing money violates the rights of hard working Americans? Did he care that altruism makes virtual slaves of the middle class, the very people he claimed to be defending? Apparently not, since he was not willing to admit that he was the real destroyer of the middle class. It was not his fault, he said. He inherited the situation, feigning innocence.

Are you now beginning to see why the President did not want to think in terms of essentials and why it was not possible for him to tell you the truth? If he were truly an honest man, he would have admitted that his philosophy was bankrupt and that socialism had failed. His policy of socialist re-distribution was the cause of the economic situation he spoke about in Kansas.

Apparently, judging from the President's words and actions, this was not the time for the truth. According to the President, it was the time for posturing, for *pretending* to be an honest critic. It was a time for telling lies and for accusing his political enemies of doing the very things that he was doing while complaining about the greed of "fat cats". The real fat cats were his friends.

On the contrary, I think it *was* the time for telling the truth. We cannot survive without it.

In his speech, the President said:

"And ever since, there's been a raging debate over the best way to restore growth and prosperity, restore balance, restore fairness. Throughout the country, it's sparked protests and political movements – from the Tea Party to the people who've been occupying the streets of New York and other cities. It's left Washington in a near-constant state of gridlock. It's been the topic of heated and sometimes colorful discussion among the men and women running for president."

It was true, the debate had been raging, but the President's words were deliberately deceiving. He was actually attempting to set the terms of the debate to favor his long-standing Marxist agenda. His use of the words, "the best way to restore growth and prosperity, restore balance, restore fairness" was intended to establish a false Marxist package deal in your mind. He wanted you to conclude with him that we needed more government controls and regulation of the economy.

First of all, Marxists did not care to "restore growth and prosperity". They have known for decades that Marxist re-distribution did no such thing. They used the words to pull you into their world of lies. They wanted you to think they were as concerned about prosperity as you were concerned. They were not; they only wanted power and they used these words to fool you into thinking they actually wanted to make things better. In addition, their use of these terms was designed to make you think they actually knew *how* to restore growth and prosperity when they knew nothing of the kind. They wanted you to think they were a vital part of the debate about prosperity and that they merely had a different view on it; that their solution, which was to create more government coercion, was just as good as other solutions such as restoring the capitalist principles of freedom.

The other terms: "restore balance, restore fairness" are also pure Marxist myths. They assume the that balance and fairness are proper goals of social policy (meaning goals of government force) and that you, like the progressives, want a balanced and fair society. What they wanted you to ignore was that their solutions for achieving balance and fairness were nothing more than coercion, more government force and that this "solution" is actually unfair and creates the terrible imbalances we were seeing in the economy.

The other false implication of this word usage was the implication that capitalism creates imbalance and unfairness which it does not. The Marxist idea of "imbalance" in capitalism means that some people become rich and others descend further into poverty. But, in capitalism, this does not actually happen. The accumulation of large amounts of capital enables the investment in larger and larger companies such as utilities, national transportation companies, etc., all of which create a higher standard of living for everyone especially the poor. Such successes result, not because of greed, but because some people work harder and/or smarter than others. Those who come up with the best solutions to human problems in a capitalist system are necessarily going to get richer than those who don't. Why shouldn't this be the case? They know how to handle money and use it wisely. The Marxist argument ignores the fact that, in capitalism, the beneficiaries of those bigger companies are the people who buy from them and that includes the poor and middle class.

The idea that capitalism is "unfair" is based upon a similar argument; that capitalism unfairly rewards people with money and punishes those without money. Again, it is a Marxist myth that this is a problem. The truth is that there is nothing unfair about a person who creates great goods for trade and gains lots of money in the process. The individual has earned it. The idea that such people should pay higher taxes because they have unfairly taken more from the system than they put into it is pure collectivist hogwash. They have, in fact, put more into the system than they receive in terms of riches. The value they have created is worth much more than the profits they made. There is no way to put a price upon the long-term benefits of a system like capitalism that is constantly improving and making peoples' lives better. What is unfair, however, is the Marxist system that rewards people by coercively putting their abler competitors out of business.

As I mentioned, in spite of these ages-old myths used by the President, it was true that the debate about a proper economic system had raged. The Tea Party phenomenon began to develop after the politicians "saved" the economy by means of a massive infusion of fiat money into the banking system, most of which went to the banking institutions that contributed the most to politicians. These were institutions that had become "over-leveraged" in mortgage derivatives bundled by the Democrats at Fannie Mae and Freddie Mac.

While the politicians insisted that TARP was necessary to "save capitalism" back in 2008, the American people gave the politicians a clear signal: "Don't do it! Don't bail out the companies that made these bad investments." Congress, after first defeating the bill to authorize TARP, came back a week later to pass it. We are still struggling with the consequences of this mistake. When the American people saw that their politicians were doing things, massive things, without their approval, the Tea Party took shape. Later, when they saw that President Obama was engaged in massive payoffs to his political cronies under the name of "stimulus" for the economy, they knew that it was time to unite against these massive violations of their rights.

However, we should not be confused about the so-called "Occupy" movement that the President mentioned. This movement was an invention of the Obama administration and the unions, not to mention the holdovers from ACORN. Union money, laundered by the administration, was behind this movement and their goal was to support the President. There was nothing grassroots about it. It was by, about and for the Obama administration...ostensibly aimed at the very people who supported the Obama administration, the crony socialists...but clearly it was an anti-capitalist movement. This movement was nothing more than a cynical effort by the unions and the President to gin up support for their legislative agenda and to instill in the American public an anti-capitalist attitude. It was an effort to create a faux-movement to "replace" and discredit the Tea Party movement.

Don't be fooled when the President insists that the "Occupy" movement was a genuine reflection of real attitudes. This so-called movement was nothing more than the President's effort to develop the pitchforks that he needed for the coming election (2012) and beyond. These people were practicing for the street riots and disruptions that would be let loose on society should the President happen to lose the election. They were also trying to bring about the "American Summer" to follow the "Arab Spring" which did so much to disrupt the Middle East.

The President also tried to blame "gridlock" for his inability to advance his fascist agenda. However, gridlock at this point in time was a result of efforts to stop the President's massive spending programs. It was, in fact, a good thing. By electing fiscal conservatives and budget hawks, conservatives were trying to block the President's efforts to move our nation further into fascism through massive spending and interference in the economy. The President blamed gridlock for blocking the progress necessary to solve our economic problems. Eventually, he saw overriding the Constitution and ruling by Executive decree to be his only way out of the gridlock that was trying to stop his cronyism and money laundering.

We have now discovered the next reason why the President did not want to speak in terms of essential principles. He had to avoid overtly voicing his own essential principles because they have consistently been rejected by the American people. These principles are those of socialism, re-distribution and forced altruism. The President's solution to the rejection of these principles was to discuss politics as if it were a matter of "our gang versus their gang". Talking about optimism, sacrifice and communities were the President's way of insinuating himself into a conversation that seemed to be "American" in nature. This deliberate effort to obfuscate principles was the only way he and the Democrats could run for election while at the same time moving the nation headlong into full-blown socialist re-distribution. If the President could turn the debate into a sort of "gang warfare" then he need not discuss principles; he need only throw dirt and mud at his opponents in an effort to "brand" them as evil while he pretended to be the enlightened protector of the middle class.

In his speech, the President avers:

"But, Osawatomie, this is not just another political debate. This is the defining issue of our time. This is a make-or-break moment for the middle class, and for all those who are fighting to get into the middle class. Because what's at stake is whether this will be a country where working people can earn enough to raise a family, build a modest savings, own a home, secure their retirement. Now, in the midst of this debate, there are some who seem to be suffering from a kind of collective amnesia. After all that's happened, after the worst economic crisis, the worst financial crisis since the Great Depression, they want to return to the same practices that got us into this mess. In fact, they want to go back to the same policies that stacked the deck against middle-class Americans for way too many years. And their philosophy is simple: We are better off when everybody is left to fend for themselves and play by their own rules."

What did the President mean when he said that some "want to return to the same practices that got us into this mess"? He should be referring to the practices of socialism since it was re-distribution of bank mortgages that caused the crisis. But the President was referring to the practices of capitalism and the people who want to return to it were Tea Party people and only a few Republicans. The President and his Occupy friends were blaming capitalism for the crisis they had created and hoped you bought into the lie. To be sure, they didn't want you to think very deeply about the causes of the crisis. That's why they cleverly accused the opposition of collective amnesia.

The President held that the "practices" of capitalism involved making money at any cost, by any means and through any deception possible. Certainly, then, he averred, these practices must have caused our financial crisis – not the practices of his best friends, the Democrats and Fannie and Freddie. Yet, this view was not new. It was one of the most long-running non-sequiturs in the history of economics. It was caused by using a false moral evaluation as the foundation for what is intended to be a "factual" conclusion; the conclusion that capitalism had failed. In fact, they were blaming capitalism for their own failures. Talk about collective amnesia.

The question of what caused our economic collapse is one for economic science, not morality. An astute analyst would ask about the specific actions men made that caused a specific economic result. Only by identifying the individual players and the specific actions they took can we arrive at an identification of the specific moral premises that caused the economic result. Moral premises, when practiced politically, can have economic consequences but it is important to understand the facts first. The President's approach starts with the premise that men will always do wrong if they are left free to act. And since capitalism leaves people free to act, then the causes of a specific bad economic result must always be capitalism. This approach obfuscates the actors, the actions and the philosophies that actually caused the collapse. It was another example of thinking in non-essentials.

The result of this thought process was deception and self-deception on the part of the President. His views of the nature of man and of capitalism were wrong and this led to a distorted opinion about the causes of the collapse. In fact, because of his own moral premises, he was the one individual still engaging in the kinds of "practices" that got us into the mess. For instance, I didn't see Tea Party people asking for more sacrifice of the taxpayer's money for the sake of people harmed by the financial collapse. I saw the President asking for more sacrifice. I didn't see Tea Party people asking that people whose loans are being foreclosed be allowed to stay in their homes. I saw the President demanding this. I didn't see Tea Party people asking for loan extensions or other forms of re-financing of unpaid mortgages. I saw the President creating programs to affect this. I didn't see Tea Party people asking for bailouts of banks and AIG and Goldman Sachs and General Motors. I saw the President bailing them out.

So who wanted to return to the practices that got us into the mess? The answer was quite simply, the President.

By now, you should have noticed that the President, in framing the debate as a sort of gang warfare, was hoping his words could create the reality he desired. The result was that everything he said wound up being true in reverse and took on the nature of a lie. When he looked for villains, he did not look at his own gang, he looked at those who would stop his gang. When making an economic analysis, he did not identify the facts; he consulted his own pre-conceived moral evaluation of capitalism. Only thinking in non-essentials will enable this form of thinking in reverse.

Yet, most of us know that wishes don't make it so and the negative economic numbers don't support the argument that the President had the solution to our economic mess. Those who made an actual effort to understand reality know that the President was the destroyer of the middle class and that the "practices" which caused the collapse were those of the President and his friends. The actual "greed" responsible for the collapse was that of people who schemed to steal the taxpayer's money by means of collectivist and class warfare policies.

Yet, he was right that this was the defining issue of his Presidency. This was a make or break moment for all of us, not just those of us in the middle class. Many of us knew then that the best way to "raise a family, build a modest savings, own a home, secure (our) retirement" was for America to move back to Constitutional liberties and capitalism. That isn't collective amnesia; that's recognizing the fact that only freedom can create the kind of prosperity necessary for the middle class to exist. Unfortunately, for the President, reality did not bend to his wishes.

The real debate that has raged for the last 200 plus years, has been between collectivist philosophies that bind man in slavery and the philosophy of the Enlightenment that declared man a free sovereign individual. In fact, this is the debate started by John Locke and the Founding Fathers. They analyzed the various forms of society and concluded that a new idea could settle the debate: a limited government that defends individual rights. The Founders knew it; some of the Tea Party members know it; the President and his looting friends were still having the debate as they muddle along in non-essentials about balance and fairness and making sure that no one can fend for themselves.

The worst financial crisis since the Great Depression was caused by the policies the President espoused while in office, the idea of "re-distribution". The critical, massive mistake; the most egregious thing that the President said in this speech was that pro-capitalists believe "we are better off when everybody is left to fend for themselves and play by their own rules." This statement shows an utter lack of understanding of what capitalism is and it justifies the fear of many that the President was a Marxist who saw capitalism as evil.

The truth is that we *are* better off when we "fend for ourselves and play by our own rules"; but it is important to understand what it means to advocate freedom against tyranny and dictatorship. The President was criticizing freedom; a concept that most credible historians have identified as the very concept that has created our prosperity. Indeed, if one believes that freedom is wrong, then one can only seek to control men and ensure that freedom of action is curtailed. The President joined forces with King George and took us back to an economic policy of sacrifice and enslavement.

The Founders and many Americans would never have described freedom using those words: "to fend for themselves". These are the words a collectivist would use to criticize freedom and capitalism. It is more of the same terminology that the President used when he talked about fairness and balance. It is based upon a hatred of the idea of "voluntary cooperation" that Rand used when describing capitalism. A collectivist would call freedom "fending for ourselves" because he wants to ensure that you view freedom as a negative, predatory concept.

Collectivists don't want you to discover that freedom means freedom of the mind. They don't want you to recognize the "voluntary cooperation" that is characteristic of capitalism. They don't want you to see yourself as "an island" responsible for your own economic results; rather they want you to view yourself as helpless without someone else's sacrifice; helpless to think, to live, to love and to enjoy life.

Collectivists think they have a better idea; the pursuit of togetherness and commonality and sacrifice, a society that will drag us screaming and kicking into the coercive imposition of altruism - with smiles and lies to make us think we are doing it voluntarily. Collectivist dogma proclaims it a crime to be proud, to stand alone; to think with your own mind and to judge based upon your values and standards. A collectivist President would attempt to be the moral authority for all people. He would cast an evil eye toward anyone acting independently. He would use non-essentials to pass judgment upon those who "play by their own rules" and he would ensure that the scales are tipped in favor of those who can't fend for themselves. Who pays for the tipping of the scale? Those who can fend for themselves.

But we can't lose sight of the full reality. Collectivism has two symbolic hands: The first is the hand held out asking for your help, reminding you with a smile that you have an obligation to help others, that we should work together to make a better world, while the other hand is picking your pocket. That's what you get for thinking collectivism is a good idea in theory.

The collectivists in our universities, who taught the President and his friends, will tell you that the intellectual enemies of mankind are the ideas of reason and freedom. They will tell you that our economic salvation can be found only in collective joining by all members of society; that the able should sacrifice to lift up the group.

They may not tell you this outright. They may actually tell you that they value reason and freedom, but their definitions of these concepts are convoluted and distorted compared to the views of the Founders. They will hold out a promise of a better tomorrow while you, the average American, know, perhaps subconsciously, that a better tomorrow, on these terms, can only come if *you* work hard while others do nothing. You, the producer, are being vilified as the cause of the nation's problems while those who do not work hard are being called the victims of your drive for profit. You'll know that the decks are stacked against you, the rules are designed to punish you and, in spite of your being punished, you are supposed to accept the "justice" that represents your enslavement. As you watch while your freedom and prosperity are slipping away, you are supposed to believe that nothing has changed, that collectivism really works and that the able sacrificing to the unable is a desirable moral ideal.

Our politicians and university professors tell us that capitalism is the problem and we need to replace it with a system that fosters sacrifice for the collective; otherwise known as social justice. Is capitalism the problem?

Capitalism, as we've discussed, is a system that fosters cooperation. People use their minds to decide which products they will purchase and which they will offer for sale. As long as each individual is free to make his own rational judgments he can constantly improve his life. On the other hand, the financial crisis was caused by the requirement that bank managers drop their rational judgment and not evaluate prospective mortgage applications on their merits. Capitalism would have required that they make a rational evaluation of each loan, identify the borrower's ability to pay and make a decision based upon the expectation that the bank would make money on the loan. This process would not have allowed the banking crisis; it would have prevented the banking crisis.

Does capitalism countenance people to play by their own rules? What does the President mean when he accuses people of playing by their own rules? The President uses the term in order to falsely equate production with theft and it results in the restriction of production and the liberation of theft. The destruction of society comes when you force people to do what government wants rather than what they want.

To let people play by their own rules is, in reality, to liberate them to use rational means to accomplish their survival. It was this that the President and his friends destroyed in 1994 with the strengthened CRA rules. The real prejudice was not that aimed at the poor or black or brown; it was the prejudice aimed at bank managers who were unfairly called racist bigots because they were making loans according to rational standards. That study we talked about that declared banks racist was later found to be flawed science.

How does an honest businessman, playing by his own rules, enable his customers to survive? He does so by means of correctly ascertaining reality and developing viable products that improve their lives. This is not dog-eat-dog but human cooperation and trade. This is not playing by your own irrational rules but playing according to reality and the requirements of survival. It is survival that capitalism makes possible, not cheating, not thieving and not lying.

By characterizing capitalism as evil, the President created for himself a powerful political weapon. By means of this prejudice against capitalism and banks, he took advantage of envious hatred to loot banks of their capital. But there is one idea that makes anti-capitalism powerful and successful as a political tool. This tool is altruism. It would not be possible to vilify capitalism were it not for the pervasive influence in society of altruism. Were it not for the moral dominance of the idea of sacrifice, there would be no argument that could be used to gain coercive power in a free society.

The President knew that whenever someone advocates free markets all he had to do was claim that unchecked capitalism would take money from the poor and put it in the hands of ruthless profit-chasers. Whenever protesters complained about massive spending by the President, all he had to do was tell us about our duty to help the poor and especially those exploited by Big Business – and that the defining issue of our time was sacrifice. Whenever people demanded that the spending stop all he had to do was accuse them of wanting to hurt the poor and take away services that help them survive in a world where jobs are lacking (due to his policies).

The truth is that the President's economic policy was nothing but song and dance that touted the value of sacrifice as a means to picking peoples' pockets. The idea that the poor need homes; that they need the "American

Dream" to be provided at the expense of people who have worked hard was a travesty and a lie. Only those people who diligently work, diligently save their money and who have the ability to pay their loans should be allowed to own homes. Only by applying a rational standard can banks make money.

Yet, the President was correct. The issue of capitalism versus regulation was a defining issue of our time and we must resolve this issue once and for all. The debate, in essence, was about morality and politics because it involved basic questions about man's nature and the purpose of government. I have written about this extensively in other books.

The discussion for us here is about the proper role of government. The basic questions include: Should government have the authority to use force against citizens in order to advance goals that are contrary to the citizens? What should happen when the actions of government conflict with the needs of human survival? Does the government have the authority to coerce people who are not criminals? What should be the role of individual rights in framing the government?

And more specifically: Did the President have a respect for the rule of law? Did he understand that the government was created to protect individual rights and that there was no authority in the Constitution (and in reality) that gives one man the power to dictate to others how they should act, which products they will choose and what they will do with the money they have earned through their own work? What is the moral justification for expropriating the money of citizens and spending it on projects and programs that the Constitution does not authorize?

At every turn, it seemed the President had an answer. But it was an answer that hung in the ether without foundation and justification. He thought it was perfectly within his realm of authority to act as the sole judge of these issues because the election gave him that authority. But it did not. His campaign proclamation to bring forth "change" did not invalidate the Constitution. His intent to engage in unilateral action violated the rules of Republican government. For a man who was supposedly a Constitutional scholar, his actions represented a strange twist on the concept of Presidential power. We did not elect him to make his own laws. We elected him to be the President of the United States, not the dictator of the United States. There were constraints on his power that he was not supposed to violate.

The President thought that in order to govern, he need only declare an "emergency" and then act unilaterally. This was one of the worst arguments for Presidential Power ever to land in the White House. Forget that this approach was an invitation to "create" the emergencies that supposedly required direct action. Forget that he was inventing emergencies virtually at will. Forget that his policies violated the principles of separation of powers and checks and balances. Forget that individual rights have gone virtually out the window. What baffled most people was that the President thought he was the only person who understood the causes of our problems (self-interest) and that he knew the only solution to be altruism and re-distribution. One could not write a serious analysis of the President's theory of Presidential power; one could only write a comedy.

Yet, this was a deadly serious issue. The President subordinated our very survival to the absolute necessity of his policies regardless of any scholarly dissent. Consider what this meant for your life: You have to endure this low economy, possibly lose or never get a job, possibly lose your home if you haven't already lost it, possibly endure runaway inflation and higher taxes, just so we can implement policies that won't work.

Capitalism means survival for our citizens and our nation. The President denigrated capitalism as if the act of trying to survive was somehow immoral. Capitalism allowed for the free flow of capital and investment into better investments that made better lives. The President called capitalists "those at the top" and he demanded that more taxes be paid by the rich while he ignored the simple fact that the rich did not have enough money to pay for the massive over-spending he had done and that he had destroyed for them the incentive to make the money to pay for the next round of re-distribution. Eventually, the money will run out. No one wants to be a slave. And, when the results of the President's policies are manifest, the President would ask for more sacrifice, not just from the rich, but from the very people he claimed to be helping: the middle class. The squeeze was on and we were the lemons.

Yet, the real tax on the middle class is not found on a tax return. It is the tax of inflation which will come down hardest on the aged and the poor. This tax is accomplished by printing fiat money to pay for the massive debt the President continues to build. New printed money added to the economy dilutes the value of existing money and this creates inflation. When that inflation in the form of higher and higher prices (called runaway inflation) hits, people will not have enough money to survive, many will not know that it was the President who did this to them.

So the talk of raising taxes on the rich, because it would do nothing to eliminate the deficit, was nothing more than rhetoric. The President was using the "bash the rich" class warfare mantra, not to expose an evil player on the scene, the rich, but to hide the real evil player, himself. The President would drag the nation down rather than build it up. He would rather create conflict and discord among Americans in order to set the stage for the system of government that creates poverty.

To further understand this, I'd like to quote another speech by the President, the speech he gave on the night he was elected in 2008:

"It's been a long time coming, but tonight, because of

what we did on this day, in this election, at this defining moment, change has come to America."

There's that "defining moment" line again, or should I say, this speech was the genesis of that defining moment that he later talked about in his Kansas speech. Since we're talking about "defining" moments, why didn't the President "define" "change" when it would have helped the voters decide?

But some of us have figured it out. His actions have shown us what change meant and we said, 'No, thank you, Mr. President." We've figured out that the defining moment the President hoped for was the moment when the American people decided to make sacrifice the motivating principle of their society; the moment when they decided to loot the wealth of those who made prosperity possible; the moment when we became a society of cannibals. That was the change he brought to America.

Many of us have also figured out that, in practice, the President's "change" meant spending taxpayer money to bailout corporations and their unions. It meant spending taxpayer money to fund the creation of new industries regardless of whether the people wanted those industries. It meant printing money which stole peoples' savings and creates the hidden tax of inflation. It meant massive government debt imposed upon people without their consent. It meant using taxpayer money to fund organizations that the government favored but which the people did not. It meant putting the competitors of friends out of business through regulations and picking winners and losers. Ours was a runaway government. This was the change the President promised.

The flaw in the President's speech in Kansas was that there will never be an end to the call for sacrifice. In spite of declining economic conditions caused by too much sacrifice, the President would call for more sacrifice. That the people were impoverished, that they were starving, poorly clothed and in poor living conditions was never blamed on the government. The government was good it was thought. It was only trying to help the poor they told us. It is an old story.

When we have eaten the productive citizens alive, we must find new scapegoats. When we've destroyed the last factory, looted the last grocery store in the name of "the people", then we'll have reached the dead end. Some might remember hearing that "the best sacrifice is total sacrifice" and they'll wonder why this idea didn't make things better. Weren't they trying to do the right thing? And some few might vaguely remember the words of the President about a defining moment when we "changed" into the "right" kind of society and we'll wonder what happened. When you remember that someone "told you so" and warned you what was coming, you'll vaguely remember that these people were considered to be bad by the administration and that they died long ago. At that point, it will be time to start eating shoe leather if you can find it.

We started this chapter by recognizing our need to have honest leaders willing to admit the truth. But when the leaders are lying to the people; when their policies are creating rather than solving the problems of the nation, a free people has only one option; and that is to vote out the people who refuse to be honest with them.

No one can "regulate" prosperity into existence. No one can manipulate a people into responding positively to coercion. No one can lie themselves into power and expect that no one will know the truth. Sooner or later, someone will mumble under his breath the complaint that the leaders are bumbling idiots.

Yet, the brutal truth is that one can't use force and "hope" for anything. One does not use force against disarmed citizens in the hope that things will get better. In order to be willing to use force against other men, a man must first hate those other men. In order to invoke policies that destroy people, one must want to destroy those people. This is not something that a person can do in ignorance. This is true of the man who gives the order, the politician who votes for it and the storm trooper who enforces it with his bayonet or pistol. No one gets to the point of harming innocent people without first deciding to harm someone. The sooner we put a stop to this madness, the sooner we will be able to restore our liberties and begin living again.

There is only one way to plant the seed of prosperity in a people and that is to leave people alone. Let them think for themselves, express their own true thoughts and live according to the truth. When we recognize this again, it will be the true defining moment for a great society.

Where is George Washington when you need him?

Bailout Bonanza

The next big mistake the administration made was to continue the bailouts. First, let's understand what a bailout is, where the idea comes from and what it is intended to accomplish. A bailout is charity for millionaires. It could be called welfare for multi-million dollar corporations. It is also an aspect of crony socialism. Don't think there wasn't a large cadre of corporate executives screaming to be "saved" while the bailouts were being considered.

To fully understand the bailouts, we must understand how businesses function and the obstacles they face. When a group of individuals operate as a private corporation, they must be constantly alert, constantly striving to be the best in their field in order to beat the competition. The corporation must operate like a well-oiled, high precision machine hitting on all cylinders and producing the maximum output. Any failure or mistake by one poorly trained or lazy individual could do serious damage to the organization or end it. That one failure may be the one weakness that competitors exploit. In fact, anything that gets in the way of top corporate efficiency could kill the company.

This is a critical point if we want to understand the principle upon which capitalism thrives and that is competition. In a competitive situation, the minutest distraction or delay can be deadly to the outcome of winning in the marketplace. Such distractions and delays threaten the survival of the company. Any factor that impedes the best production, the best management and the highest profits could be deadly to the company and the survival of the employees who work for it.

These deadly factors could be something other than an internal laggard. They could also be government regulations and other unnecessary rules, onerous taxes and crony capitalism that uses government to destroy the competitors of the government's favorites. It consists of trade unions that subvert the relationship between a company and its employees. All of these factors create tremendous obstacles to the company's attainment of the highest production levels and the best quality.

Simply put, the only rule for the organization is: provide value. But how this value is provided and how much value is achieved is the province of the art of management. If a company succeeds at pleasing the customer, it is rewarded with profits. If it fails, or is forced to fail by government or unions it must go out of business, take whatever investment capital it has left and invest it in an entirely new business.

In fact, the so-called "saviors" of our economy using bailouts have a decidedly false view of corporate bankruptcy. Going out of business is not a dead end; it is the beginning of a new process that applies left-over capital to a new purpose. It revitalizes that capital and puts it to work toward a better idea. In fact, when a business folds, what it is really doing is discarding a bad idea, releasing employees to find jobs in profitable businesses and starting a new process of more intelligently using capital to begin value creation again. Companies such as Bain Capital provided tremendous benefits to the economy because their basic goals are to re-organize companies and make them profitable again, or when this is not possible, such companies ensure that whatever is left of the failing company can quickly be put to productive use again.

Contrary to the views of anti-capitalists, businesses are not about doing evil. They are about value and positive living. In fact, they can *only* be about value and positive living. The idea that business owners and managers seek to exploit the workers, that they deceive customers, that they only want to steal production and leave the employees destitute is a lie told by those who don't understand what it takes to manage a successful company. A great company hires the best people and pays them well. It trains them and sets the company Mission toward a positive goal. Employees, making what they are worth, will work hard, develop pride in their abilities, lead better lives, enjoy their free time and love their families.

The belief that a government has the authority to issue bailouts is based on the idea that government should manipulate the actions of men to improve economic conditions. The premise is that business organizations represent a set of levers that can be intelligently manipulated to produce a better outcome. If one industry is getting too powerful, then the government can shrink it down to size by taxing or fining it at a higher level than its competitors.

Bailouts do not work and there is no good outcome except in the short-term. While damage is done to the people who provide the money for the bailout, politicians only talk about the boost that the bailout gave to the corporation. It considers this boost a success but the bailout only mitigated the eventual demise of the company. The bailout actually created distortions in the marketplace and left the managers of the bailed out company with no cognitive indication of how their decisions will affect profits. Competitors who did not receive bailouts are benefited because their decisions will be immediately reflected in their bottom line and they will know how to react to the changing marketplace. The best thing for the bailed out company to do is give back the bailout money so it can get back to a position where the bottom line is the only indicator of its success. Politics and cronyism are not indicators of corporate success...but of a corrupt corporate culture.

The only exception that I'm aware of was the previous Chrysler bailout a few decades ago. In that situation, an exceptional CEO took over the company and successfully steered it to recovery. He took the bailout as if it were a loan and proceeded to make the changes necessary to save the company and pay the government back. After much hard work and intelligent planning, Chrysler was saved. Today, that will not happen because most businesspeople who clamor for a bailout do not have the intelligence, ability or desire to actually compete in the economy. They would rather ride the company boat as long as the tide is up, but they'll bail out themselves as soon as the obvious becomes known; that bailouts are not a solution for a failing company. Bankruptcy is.

Today, President Obama touts the GM bailout as a success while the company continues to survive on the "charity" of the US taxpayer who no longer wants to buy their cars. What can you expect when government gives a company a bunch of money it did not earn? These bailouts were given to GM specifically to protect the jobs of one of the President's biggest contributors among the powerful unions. You can be sure that the money will be wasted.

In fact, you can be sure the bailout is failing when you see a union thug (who visits the President every week) on "Face the Nation" telling you about his concern for the jobs of Americans, smiling like an all-American boy, honest and true. Few people notice that his whole existence is made possible by stepping on the backs, not only of the union members forced to work under him, but of the American taxpayers. The fact is that this very individual is responsible for GM failing in the first place. That he pretends to be an all-American boy (rather than the thug he is) proves that there is corruption at the highest levels of our government.

Trade Union Bonanza

When President Obama decided to "save" GM, it was because of his ideological support of unions. Trade unions protected by government are another form of cronyism that does tremendous harm to workers and corporations.

The trade union muscles in on the employee's pay and promises collective bargaining in situations where it is not necessary. A trade union subverts the goals of the company and turns the corporate priority from the practice of making a profit to that of providing welfare for unproductive employees. Union leaders think it is ok for unproductive employees to subvert the company by being argumentative, hyper-legal and anti-capitalist. Yet, all of these attitudes require that the managers of the company find ways to mitigate the damage done to the organization by the union.

Remember what I wrote about productivity above and how one unproductive or incompetent employee can ruin a company. Now, imagine a situation where the union forces wages so high that the company is no longer competitive. The solution offered by the union leaders is to have the government declare the corporation too important to fail.

But this is not exactly what Obama did. As he negotiated with GM, he must certainly have been told about the harm the union was doing to the company. The lack of production, the drinking on the job, the lack of cooperation, the grievance process, firing procedures that protected union jobs worked to destroy the company's productive posture and gave competitors a chance to gain market share. His solution was to fire some executives (which was unprecedented) and save the union. For Obama, the union was too big to fail.

I have been a member of two labor unions during my long career. The first, when I was very young, decided to strike for higher pay for its members. Eventually, after many months on strike, the union won the labor rates for which it held out. Once we got back to work, the corporation engaged in massive layoffs because, during the strike, competitors of the company had managed to take away most of the customers. I lost my job.

I was in another union for about 11 years at a major transportation company. In this case, the company, many decades before, had decided it wanted to avoid union agitation and, rather than fight unionization, invited the union to represent its employees. Yet, many of my fellow union members did not like the union. The union "bosses" acted like thugs and the company, over the years, endured several strikes. This left room for Federal Express to start up without paying union wages.

It seems that everyone is saying "unions can be good for the workers" but I think it is time we question the roles that unions have played in society. One of the most eloquent critics of unions was the little-known economist Ludwig von Mises from Austria. Below, I list some of the "problems" of unions and inject some of his most prescient criticisms:

1. Unions can gain no improvements in wages, benefits or working conditions that companies would not already be able to provide. If the business was not already successful and earning a significant profit, there would be no interest among union bosses to unionize the employees. In other words, unions would not exist without a strong capitalist system from which to derive dues.
a. Ludwig von Mises: "The union members are not conscious of the fact that their fate is tied up with the flowering of their employers' enterprises." – Planning for Freedom p. 91

2. Unions tend to agitate in order to justify their existence.
a. Ludwig von Mises: "Strikes, sabotage, violent action and terrorism of every kind are not economic means. They are destructive means, designed to interrupt the movement of economic life. They are weapons of war which must inevitably lead to the destruction of society." – Socialism p. 307

3. Unions are a defacto government regulation of businesses (a form of crony socialism).
a. Ludwig von Mises: "The labor unions aim at a monopolistic position on the labor market. But once they have attained it, their policies are restrictive and not monopoly price policies. They are intent upon restricting

the supply of labor in their field without bothering about the fate of those excluded." – Human Action p. 374 - 377

4. Unions put companies out of business. They force employers to raise wages that often put the company in an uncompetitive position. The company has no choice but to close the factory, move to another state or move overseas to remain profitable.

5. Unions support socialist/progressive platforms because progressive politicians want union votes. In return for votes, politicians allow unions the power to coerce businesses. Unions also tend to support bills and legislative measures that raise taxes, give them more power in negotiations and remove consent from employees and business owners. In the case of government unions, the government enables unions to demand benefits and pay raises regardless of whether the union members are doing a good job. These "advances" for the working man are merely excuses to launder those tax increases to the union bosses by means of increased union dues. This is re-distribution disguised as a contractual benefit. It is a welfare program for people who do very little.

6. Unions destroy worker/company relations because they create a "we versus them" attitude. Unions must be collectivist in nature. They need to create a "group think" where union members consider themselves part of a fight or struggle to gain more power over time and skim more profits. Union members are often discouraged from having a stake in the success of the company.

7. Unions often say they favor the little guy. This is not true; in many cases Big Unions favor Big Business and Big Government. They create crony socialism where government is used to benefit all parties and restrict competition from non-union companies.

8. Labor unions tend to strongly oppose the introduction of new technologies and more productive machinery because they mean that the company can improve production while using fewer workers. Instead, unions look for opportunities to create unproductive jobs, duplicate jobs and patronage jobs in order to swell membership rolls and collect more money in dues and pension plans. These actions lower production, raise product prices and harm the competitive position of businesses. Sometimes, in order to use the new highly productive technologies, companies must move to "right to work" states or out of the country which reduces local employment.

9. Labor unions take the credit for higher wages and this tends to justify violence and otherwise illegal practices.
a. Ludwig von Mises: "As people think that they owe to unionism their high standard of living, they condone violence, coercion, and intimidation on the part of unionized labor and are indifferent to the curtailment of personal freedom inherent in the union-shop and closed-shop clauses." – Planning for Freedom p. 153

10. Unions restrict the division of labor. Any improved business process which requires new higher skills from

employees is resisted and the company is often forced to provide unproductive jobs for those displaced by division of labor improvements.

a. Ludwig von Mises: "No social cooperation under the division of labor is possible when some people or unions of people are granted the right to prevent by violence and the threat of violence other people from working." – Planned Chaos p. 127

11. Unions seek political power, using government, so they can monopolize and control labor and hold that control over corporations and taxpayers.

a. Ludwig von Mises: "The cornerstone of trade unionism is compulsory membership." – Socialism p. 435

12. The power of unions comes from their government-protected ability to strike which is a method of stopping production and harming businesses and jobs.

a. Ludwig von Mises: "The weapon of the trade union is the strike. It must be borne in mind that every strike is an act of coercion, a form of extortion, a measure of violence directed against all who might act in opposition to the strikers' intentions." – Socialism p. 435

b. Ludwig von Mises: "The policy of strike, violence, and sabotage can claim no merit whatever for any improvement in the worker's position." – Socialism p. 437

13. Unions are tied to capitalism and the success of capitalist organizations, yet union bosses routinely propagandize against capitalism. They express false Marxist views of capitalism and use the moral argument

against capitalist profits and production improvements. They prejudice union members against their capitalist employers and create discord even in situations where the employers are trying to improve the strength and profitability of the company.

14. When possible or necessary, unions have no problem compelling membership through practices like card check. This puts a union thug behind each voter to ensure that he/she votes the "right" way.

15. Unions have less regard for member rights than they do for maintaining the status quo. In many cases grievances are settled in complete disregard for the merits of the case. Union bosses sometimes trade grievance settlements for other "considerations".

16. Unions have an incentive to keep poorly performing employees on the job and many unions have little regard for whether the member actually does a good job. This destroys productivity, encourages a cynical work ethic and undermines the ability of management to engineer a productive enterprise.

17. Unions tend to squander the money they collect in dues and pension plan payments. This forces them to "buy" politicians who will request bailouts from government to make up shortfalls. The taxpayer is rewarding them for their loss of trust among their members.

18. Union leaders (and many politicians) demand that we never question their motives but always question the motives of people whose productive and organizational abilities provide the union dues and pension payments. They tell us that their goal is to help people and bring about "social justice" while the motives of corporate managers is to steal money that would not exist but for those very corporate managers. Additionally, it is the corporate managers, not the union leaders, who provide the jobs, industrial plants and capital investments that make possible the magnificent products that make our lives better. They tell you that it is proper for them to use force against those corporate managers but improper for anyone to question union leaders about what they do with the billions of dollars they, the union leaders, "earn".

I think that most people who work in a union shop will recognize many of these "problems" with unions. Certainly, the President relied heavily on the support of unions in his two Presidential campaigns. Unions represent one of his biggest crony supporters and his administration did everything possible to help unions grow as well as maintain their power.

How do unions get away with their cronyism? It is really very simple; they are morally exempt from the rules. They rely on altruism, the idea that their goals are good and their enemies are evil makes it possible for them to appeal to government for special consideration. In fact, over the years, the union bosses have lost the lustre of good works. Scandals, bullying and out right treachery have caused union members to lose their respect for unionism and today the only factor that keeps unions powerful is their practice of investing huge funds to buy politicians.

Unions are on the wane because many workers have learned that corporations, for the most part, are not as evil and treacherous as they have been portrayed. Many of them provide good benefits, good pay and they treat their employees well. It is seldom true that honest workers need to be defended by unions. The result is that when asked if they want to work in a union shop, talented workers would prefer to rely on the strength of their individual skills and knowledge without joining a collective. They prefer to be treated fairly by their employer and fair treatment is most often what they have found. It is the marginally productive individual who puts very little of himself into his work who finds that he is less valued as an employer who thinks he benefits by joining with others.

The President hitched his horses to unions who exploited this second group of marginally productive workers for their own benefit and he made a sort of "deal with the devil" in order to benefit politically. It was the effort to help unions politically that enabled the shrinking unions to stay viable.

The Resurgence of Keynes

John Maynard Keynes is a name few modern people will recognize. Sometimes they will hear it referred to as Keynesianism in discussions of economic theory but still they may not know much about what is being discussed.

"Keynes was born in Cambridge and attended King's College, Cambridge, where he earned his degree in mathematics in 1905. He remained there for another year to study under Alfred Marshall and Arthur Pigou, whose scholarship on the quantity theory of money led to Keynes's Tract on Monetary Reform many years later. After leaving Cambridge, Keynes took a position with the civil service in Britain. While there, he collected the material for his first book in economics, Indian Currency and Finance, in which he described the workings of India's monetary system. He returned to Cambridge in 1908 as a lecturer, then took a leave of absence to work for the British Treasury. He worked his way up quickly through the bureaucracy and by 1919 was the Treasury's principal representative at the peace conference at Versailles. He resigned because he thought the Treaty of Versailles was overly burdensome for the Germans."[9]

'[Keynes] returned to Cambridge to resume teaching. A prominent journalist and speaker, Keynes was one of the famous Bloomsbury Group of literary greats, which also included Virginia Woolf and Bertrand Russell. At the 1944

---

[9] http://www.econlib.org/library/Enc/bios/Keynes.html (The Concise Encyclopedia of Economics)

Bretton Woods Conference, where the International Monetary Fund was established, Keynes was one of the architects of the postwar system of fixed exchange rates. In 1925 he married the Russian ballet dancer Lydia Lopokova. He was made a lord in 1942. Keynes died on April 21, 1946, survived by his father, John Neville Keynes, also a renowned economist in his day. (brackets mine)

"Keynes became a celebrity before becoming one of the most respected economists of the century when his eloquent book The Economic Consequences of the Peace was published in 1919. Keynes wrote it to object to the punitive reparations payments imposed on Germany by the Allied countries after World War I. The amounts demanded by the Allies were so large, he wrote, that a Germany that tried to pay them would stay perpetually poor and, therefore, politically unstable. We now know that Keynes was right. Besides its excellent economic analysis of reparations, Keynes's book contains an insightful analysis of the Council of Four (Georges Clemenceau of France, Prime Minister David Lloyd George of Britain, President Woodrow Wilson of the United States, and Vittorio Orlando of Italy).

"Keynes wrote: 'The Council of Four paid no attention to these issues [which included making Germany and Austro-Hungary into good neighbors], being preoccupied with others—Clemenceau to crush the economic life of his enemy, Lloyd George to do a deal and bring home something which would pass muster for a week, the **President to do nothing that was not just and right'** (chap.

6, para. 2).

"In the 1920s Keynes was a believer in the quantity theory of money (today called Monetarism). His writings on the topic were essentially built on the principles he had learned from his mentors, Marshall and Pigou. In 1923 he wrote *Tract on Monetary Reform,* and later he published *Treatise on Money,* both on Monetary Policy. His major policy view was that the way to stabilize the economy is to stabilize the price level, and that to do that the government's central bank must lower Interest Rates when prices tend to rise and raise them when prices tend to fall.

"Keynes's ideas took a dramatic change, however, as Unemployment in Britain dragged on during the interwar period, reaching levels as high as 20 percent. Keynes investigated other causes of Britain's economic woes, and *The General Theory of Employment, Interest and Money* was the result.

"Keynes's *General Theory* revolutionized the way economists think about economics. It was pathbreaking in several ways, in particular because it introduced the notion of aggregate demand as the sum of consumption, Investment, and government spending; and because it showed (or purported to show) that full employment could be maintained only with the help of government spending. Economists still argue about what Keynes thought caused high unemployment. Some think he attributed it to wages that take a long time to fall. But Keynes actually wanted wages not to fall, and in fact advocated in the *General Theory* that wages be kept stable. A general cut in wages, he argued, would decrease income, consumption, and aggregate demand. This would offset any benefits to output that the lower price of labor might have contributed.

"Why shouldn't government, thought Keynes, fill the shoes of business by investing in public works and hiring the unemployed? *The General Theory* advocated deficit spending during economic downturns to maintain full employment. Keynes's conclusion initially met with opposition. At the time, balanced budgets were standard practice with the government. But the idea soon took hold and the U.S. government put people back to work on public works projects. Of course, once policymakers had taken deficit spending to heart, they did not let it go."[10]

Keynesian principles coincide easily with the idea of a "socialized" government; where all decisions are based upon "the good of society" and where all forms of coercion are within the government's authority. Keynesianism advocates an essentially fascist government where citizens own property but government decides what they should do. These principles release into society (to function with impunity) looters, thugs and thieves who use the gullibility of the American public to proclaim that they are saving a difficult situation by means of their coercive actions. These people have no intention of saving

[10] Ibid

anything. They are actually using the situation to loot every ounce of money produced by honest citizens. Keynesianism is the looters' argument made by people who will leave us all with empty bank accounts.

Keynes accepted as fact the Marxist idea that capitalism creates unfairness and other disparities that must be corrected by government. Such "disparities" as wealth accumulation and monopolies require that government act to fix "macro-economic" distortions. It establishes the lie that government economists have the ability to analyze and identify these disparities and recommend solutions. Keynesian economics brought the birth of the technocrat who thought he knew better what people should do with their lives and who ushered in an era of coercive "solutions" that did not work.

However, classical economists such as Ludwig von Mises saw the problems of Keynesianism and sought to warn us that the market did not respond well to coercive measures; he taught that government intervention actually created the disparities that Keynesian economists and politicians claim to be fixing. Classical economists told us that there is nothing wrong with capital accumulation; it actually makes bigger and better businesses possible. They told us that monopolies were virtually impossible in a truly free market. They even pointed out that only government can create monopolies by barring entry into a field. They countenanced free markets where individual rights were honored and protected by government.

Classical economists will also tell you that any form of government interference in the marketplace causes distortions which affect the ability of businesses to earn profits. For the sake of "social justice" Keynesians will make it difficult for some businesses to survive and easier for others, all of which causes the very problems and distortions that the government claims to be today's "emergency". An example of this is the intervention that brought about the mortgage crisis precipitated by Fannie Mae and Freddie Mac in 2008. This was an entirely government-manufactured crisis made possible only by government manipulation of bank lending practices.

As a Keynesian, President Obama brought Keynesian technocrats into government who cavalierly dismissed the American businesspeople to the point of insulting them and treating them as virtual slaves. This attitude is a result of Keynesian and Marxist principles that assign to bureaucrats the ability to violate the right to property. The result of this attitude is that the President's men had no problem with "solutions" that involved coercive measures against once free people. If something was wrong, in their minds, that means someone should fix it; and that "someone" was always government. Little did they realize that all they had to do was stop tinkering with the economy and free people would make the right decisions for themselves. Little did they realize that the problem is not capitalism; but their tinkering with the economy.

While reading the book, "The Escape Artists", I noticed

this attitude to be rampant among the President's advisors. These men, the President's key advisors from 2009 to 2016, acted like desperate dictators clamoring to control the entire economy. They acted as if the economy could only be saved by finding villains to vilify, parading a few executives in handcuffs, engaging in lots of anti-business propaganda and imposing rampant regulation to ensure that businessmen feared the President. None of them said, "Wait a minute. This isn't our proper role. We don't have the authority to violate individual rights. We aren't doing the right thing when we issue decrees. This isn't how law is made in America." It didn't matter that businessmen were innocent of wrong doing, that they haven't broken any laws or that they bend over backwards to follow government regulations. What mattered is that someone else be blamed for the consequences of government action (the subprime crisis) and that the victims be vilified publicly in order to maintain the (false) image that the government is working for the people. The basic attitude was that, now that the President was in control, businesspeople were slaves to the state. The only important issue for them was saving the President's political skin and making sure he wasn't blamed for his corruption and that of his cronies.

How did we get to the state in the U.S.A. where politicians and Presidential advisors can do anything they want and say anything they want? How did we get to a point where the Constitution is not even an after-thought? I think the answer to this question will prove enlightening, especially for those among us who were then confused by everything coming out of the government.

The administration's basic approach was philosophical dishonesty. The government under Obama held that truth is what people believe, that you have to create the truth by repeating lies; and that people vote according to which party spends the most money distorting the facts – and that bailouts actually bail out companies if people believe it. This philosophical premise is known as subjectivism, the idea that reality is created by a collective mind and that the only thing needed is to educate the people so their beliefs will create the reality the manipulators hope for.

What do they hope? They hope that wishing makes it so, that whims will create the truth, that we can continue robbing Peter to pay Paul and that there will never be any consequences for their robberies. They hope that if the people will just believe it, then all their evasions of reality, all their coercive measures, all their lies and distortions will somehow cause reality to bend to their will.

I've said for years that progressives must engage in "reverse think" in order to succeed. They must tell us everything in reverse... because they don't know how to affect reality except by lying to people – and many times, they don't even know that they are thinking in reverse. Just listen to them and you'll see that everything out of their mouths is true in reverse. They tell you that capitalism has caused our financial crisis, that the real cause, government, must be given more power, that the solution (that has not worked), government coercion, must be engaged even more (rather than stopped), that capitalists are thieves, that the rich are not paying their fair share...all of these "facts" are actually "lies".

To quote from John Young's Blog:

"Remember, as the Declaration of Independence noted, governments derive their JUST powers from the consent of the governed. Obviously, I cannot give someone else "consent" to do something that is highly illegal for me to do as well. That's why people who hire assassins go to jail just as if they had conducted the assassination personally. Well, then … as I have no right to go taking away other people's stuff, I can't give government "consent" to do so on my behalf, either. Thus, the entire Keynesian premise flies in the face of the underlying tenets of our system of government and is ipso facto UNJUST."[11]

This last is the TRUTH. It is the very truth that the President would like to ignore because, were he to acknowledge the fact that his policies cannot work, that his words cannot make them work and that he cannot get away with stealing peoples' money; not only would his inner universe collapse but, in his mind, so would the entire universe.

---

[11] http://yjohn.wordpress.com/2009/01/28/obama-keynes-and-bailout-ii/

The President's belief that capitalism has created disparities in wealth is an excellent example to prove my point, another example of reverse think.

John Young's Blog responds again:

"In any free market, there will always be natural disparities in wealth. Some people are smarter than others, some people are more industrious than others, and some people are just plain lucky. Sometimes very bright people find themselves following a calling or cause that doesn't pay well. Some people just don't care about money. Others are incredibly acquisitive. This is just the way the world works, and government shouldn't be interfering to make things work any differently."[12]

And this is the point about the bailouts. The President and his men act as if this country was their possession to manipulate at will. They act as if they had the right to just move any amount of money around and give it to anyone they want...as long as they have an "emergency" that allows them to ignore the facts of reality. They act as if the election had given the President a mandate to ignore the Constitution, that they could decide which men will receive good treatment and which will be excoriated. They advanced measure after measure of highly questionable and immoral decrees that other people would have to follow under pain of punishment. They advanced the idea that people should sacrifice for the

---

[12] Ibid

sake of the collective, or else. They believed that profits are evil and that men will always do what is wrong unless they, the most insulting characters around, can dictate to them what is proper. Men who had never worked an actual day in their lives were telling those of us who had worked for many years how to conduct our business – and it is considered proper that we gave them the time of day. In any other situation in our country's past, they'd have to sit on the street and beg for other peoples' money. Not today.

"Bailouts are an ideologically-based idea that has been stripped of its ideological context by intellectuals in order to mainstream the idea that they are merely rational thought. This intellectual mind trick has a sinister influence on a society of people who do not realize that bailouts are essentially fascist/socialist in nature. They are a piece of the puzzle that represents an effort to fool people into accepting dictatorship. If you accept bailouts, you can accept more bailouts. And you must also accept the way things are done by government. You must accept political bribes, graft and unconstitutional acts. You must accept the immoral as moral and you must learn to think of everything in reverse. When you hear a lie, it is social truth. When you tell the truth it is a capitalist lie. When you accept higher taxes, you are engaging in order to solve problems. When you cannot afford to live, it is Justice. But don't worry; our vital industries will continue to function and provide us with what we need. Our sacrifice will save us. That we can't afford a car that does not work very well is an indication that our government is forcing us to be socially responsible (That is a lie too)."

Sacrifice, Sacrifice, Sacrifice – The Cult of Sacrifice

That a single individual (who had not earned his millions by productive work) had been given the power to impose upon us his singular philosophy of sacrifice is an indication of how much "reverse think" was rampant in society during Obama's term. That we thought that a person (dedicated to forced altruism) could actually make the right decision on any issue should have made any thinking Americans pause.

How can sacrifice be the answer to every economic problem? When has it ever been successfully implemented in society and succeeded in creating a vibrant economy? Certainly not in the Dark Ages ruled by Christianity. Certainly not in Soviet Russia, Nazi Germany, Fascist Italy, Communist China and Communist Cuba to name a few. All of these countries glorified and implemented sacrifice.

Yet, we are to consider that a man who has shown himself capable of only making this one decision to foster sacrifice on all issues...is qualified to lead a country built upon the principle of freedom and self-interest? Can we expect anything other than a destruction of our society at his hands? His every decision was to re-distribute; his every action was to demand sacrifice, to regulate, to stimulate, to ease monetary printing, to punish the successful and to make sure his friends are not touched by his decisions. This was the essence of the man we elected. What did you expect, the roaring twenties?

Were the President's Czars and regulators beholden to a principle such as individual rights? No, it would have been ludicrous to ask them to be throttled by restrictions on their actions; they were too busy fighting against the "evil" profit-seekers, against the very people who built our computers and cell phones and iPads. They were too busy destroying the symbols of success because they considered successful people to be an evil conspiracy to steal. Yet, look who did the stealing...those very Czars and regulators.

The President's principle of sacrifice held that it was proper for men to sacrifice for the sake of others. He obtained his authority to force men to sacrifice, not from the Constitution (which prohibited theft and coercion), but from God and a democratic vote that was presumed (by him) to be a repudiation of the Constitution. The President's altruism, which also fostered the Marxist premise (from each according to his ability to each according to his need) is what we supposedly voted for. At least, that's what he and Michelle believed. More reverse think.

The President ignored his job description. The Presidency was not about being the re-distributor-in-chief or the altruist-in-chief or the regulator-in-chief or the Keynesian-in-chief. His job was to execute the laws of the land and to do so in a way that was Constitutional. It would not have been difficult to just leave people free to solve their own problems.

The founders knew that future leaders would attempt to create emergencies that enabled them to take power and violate the Constitution and they sought to prevent it by creating a system that would span generations before it could be totally invalidated.

The President has been only one of those few leaders who attempted to circumvent the Constitution. And reality showed that he could not create a new definition of fairness that requires unfairness. He could not invent of new type of government without having to suffer the consequences that have always come from the old types (fascism, socialism, communism, welfare-statism). Those consequences are various forms of destruction.

It was not within the President's authority to take money from American taxpayers and give it to anyone – especially people who had donated heavily to his campaign. As John Young's Blog tells us, theft is illegal. The bailouts were not only fruitless, they were immoral. Not only did they save some companies from having to compete, they put off the eventual debacle into the future – a debacle that will be caused by the President's policies. Not only have the President's pro-sacrifice views empowered immoral, non-productive people like his advisors, but they are destroying the successful people who got wealthy through their own diligence.

President Obama's Press Conference in Hawaii can provide us with a "light-bulb" moment about the President's sacrificial mindset. It provides a microcosm of insight into a pattern of thinking that has characterized mankind for centuries to its detriment. I call it the Cult of Sacrifice. Here is the President's statement regarding the "need" for Congress to pass his "American Jobs Act":

"This doesn't require radical changes to America or its way of life. It just means that we spread out the sacrifice across every sector so that it's fair; so that people don't feel as if once again people who are well connected, people who have lobbyists, special interests get off easy, and the burden is placed on middle-class families that are already struggling. So if other countries can do it, we can do it — and we can do it in a responsible way.

"I'm not going to comment on whether I'd veto a particular bill until I actually see a bill, because I still hold out the prospect that there's going to be a light-bulb moment where everybody says 'Ah-ha! Here's what we've got to do.'"

As the President indicated, "what we've got to do" is sacrifice, spread out the suffering so that no one person suffers too much. Yet, one thing he overlooked is that the debt of this country cannot be dealt with if you took all the money made by the richest in America. In fact, the debt is so massive that all those riches would barely put a dent into the deficit. Even spreading out the suffering would accomplish no negligible benefit to our society, more sacrifice will make no difference to our debt or to any of the many invented problems created by the administration.

Some people thought that the President's logic was flawless. Certainly, as patriotic Americans we all want to make things better in our society. And, some thought, considering the present circumstances, that our leaders were only trying to encourage Americans to do their part to lift society out of the doldrums. But, I think the President's remarks were nothing more than a ritualized (in other words, automatized) response that has been repeatedly imposed upon mankind for centuries – and it has never worked. In fact, it is a form of "sleight of hand" where the President offered great benefits to the people if they would only sacrifice; but, historically, in other similar cases, those benefits were never accomplished. The only thing we did was lose people, energy and time.

In fact, our deficit problem was created by the very same thinking in which the President was asking us to engage. He asked us to sacrifice for our fellow man. Yet, isn't that mindset, the mindset of sacrificing, the very idea that caused the deficit in the first place? Indeed, the trigger for the economic collapse, the subprime crisis was caused by former President Clinton who asked the banks to sacrifice so that more people could buy homes. The result was a massive number of foreclosures; and those people who got homes then are now sacrificing whatever money they have left to the banks that were decimated by the original sacrifice. It seems that someone has figured out how to use sacrifice to convince people to re-distribute lots of money. It is an old game.

Along the way, President Obama's biggest supporters have become exceedingly wealthy by taking in more sacrifice from the tax payers, creating a crony socialist scheme that rewarded his supporters with stimulus dollars so they could do it all over again in 2012. Everyone got rich but the taxpayers who were sacrificing. This is the ancient Cult of Sacrifice made modern.

Ayn Rand, in her novel Atlas Shrugged was correct in her assessment of cronyism. In the universe she created, it was the crony socialists who were using the language of duty, of collective salvation and of love in order to justify their thefts; in short, the language of sacrifice. They used this language to condition society to the necessity of sacrifice, all the while, destroying their industrial enemies in order to keep their grip on power. As each new producer rose up, he was immediately seized upon as by vultures and eaten alive by laws, government programs and regulations. Each new sacrifice was supposedly engaged for the good of society, to save society, to get us out of the doldrums. And the argument was always: "we should spread the sacrifice around".

In spite of the fact that Atlas Shrugged was a fictional story, today we are seeing it come to life as if it were prophesy. And, as happened in Ayn Rand's fictional universe, our universe keeps descending into more poverty and more calls for sacrifice. How could she get it so right? How could she know that cronyism is the hallmark of collectivism, of communism, of socialism and of fascism? Her answer was "Identify the dominant philosophy of a society and you can predict its future."[13] Today, the dominant philosophy of society is "The Cult of Sacrifice".

Today, cronyism has exposed itself as a "bubble" and it is ready to burst. The entire house of cards built by the President and a long line of other preachers of sacrifice, a house made up of "looters" as Ayn Rand would call them, is beginning to collapse around the nation. The cronies have taken over the economy and no one is safe until the American people put a stop to it. They must restore the Constitution by limiting the power of the President.

Many people know that the President was lying with virtually every sentence he uttered as candidate and President, and that nothing he said or did brought about an economic resurgence. His words were more of the same; more calls for the very sacrifice that got us into the situation. What is the Cult of Sacrifice; and how is it destroying us? It is not something new, but something very old, like a dusty old skeleton dug up after centuries in the sand...propped up as the source of life when it is merely old and dead.

Let's begin at the beginning; somewhere in a distant past, before history was being written. It was within this past that we can see the remnants of the Cult of Sacrifice. Imagine that archaeologists have just dug up a group of people who had not gone through the Industrial

---

13 quoted in "Ayn Rand – The Prophesy of Atlas Shrugged

Revolution, whose level of knowledge was miniscule compared to ours. These people knew so little that they interpreted everything they saw from a primitive perspective. They saw the influence of "spirits" everywhere and their most fundamental principle was that there were two dimensions of reality, the world of the spirits and the world of reality in which they lived. One realm was superior, active and real (the world of the spirits) and the other was full of fear, terror and catastrophe (the reality in which they lived). These people yearned for the paradise of the spiritual world and wanted to escape the drudgery of the real.

Everywhere the archaeologists dig, they uncover bodies without heads in one place, and in another place, heads without bodies. They find children buried at the cornerstones of buildings and the tombs of kings with hundreds of dead "attendants" including people, animals, chariots of war and even whole horses. They find a "cemetery" with bodies thrown in as in a mass grave and they find votive offerings with statues of ancient gods whose names are long lost to history. Everywhere, they find the Cult of Sacrifice.

The gods and spirits were everywhere for the men in this society, influencing their daily lives and sometimes even raining down disaster, hurricane and earthquake as punishment for not honoring them. The archaeologists find layer upon layer of dust in the village and layer upon layer of buildings built upon older buildings as if periodic destruction came to this society. And with each destruction layer, they found more bodies.

For these people, the spirits lived, not only in the heavens, but in the animals and objects of nature, everything had an animating spirit and everything that happened on this earth was influenced by the interventions of these spirits. Understanding what the gods demanded was a daunting task that could only have been accomplished by the priest/rulers who presumed to have a deep connection to the gods and spirits. They were the leaders of this society.

We must understand that these people had no science. They had no view of reality that informed them of cause and effect and they had only their trust in their leaders. If their leaders told them that in order to save society, they must offer up their children in sacrifice to the gods, they believed it. If they were told that in order to ensure that earthquakes did not destroy their buildings, they had to bury a living child at the cornerstone of each building. If they were told that the gods were angry at them and could only be appeased through the brutal murder of some of their citizens, they believed such sacrifice was necessary. If they were told that, as servants of the king, they must continue their service by being buried with him upon his death, they believed that as soon as they died en masse they would attain a new life of service to the king.

This new archaeological find, however, is not so different from other finds which have been discovered all over the world, on every continent, in virtually every country and river bank on the planet. And, as we examine the writing of recent history and explore our planet, we see strains of human sacrifice, even up to modern times. The brutal truth is that the Cult of Sacrifice has informed the lives of people for century upon century.

Throughout these many centuries, most men believed that all causes were enacted by the gods and all men must live in their service. Did any of these men notice that sometimes their devout sacrifice did not accomplish the end they sought? Yes, but they were told that they had not sacrificed enough. Did any of them question their religion for asking them to give up their highest values? Yes, they were soon offered up as the next to be sacrificed (See Diagoras). Did any of them offer their own bodies in order to save the lives of their children? Yes, but they were told that only the sacrifice of children could appease the gods. At each questioning of the wisdom of the ruling elites, there was an argument ready and one thing they did not question: the belief that the gods existed and that they could rain devastation upon them.

The cult of sacrifice was so engrained in men during past ages that even today men believe they have to sacrifice to God or Allah in order to live moral lives. Sacrifice, today called altruism, is a remnant of the human sacrifice that was practiced by our ancient forebears. And all the negatives of ancient ritual sacrifice are with us today in lost human energy, lost dignity and lost love; in devastated societies and people resigned to suffering and death. It has come down to us from religion and those philosophers influenced by Plato who preached a two-dimensional universe.

Ritual is the scripted reenactment of mythological tales about the lives of the gods. Ritual is the ancient version of moral thinking. In fact, ritual is the method by which ancient leaders kept the "people" in line, controlled their activities and instituted their sacrificing. A ritual was both a commemoration of the lives of the gods and a moral lesson on how to act at all times. Ritual told men how to live, how to be god-like. Ritual always included collectivism, obedience and sacrifice and was the means through which ancient rulers earned their booty or "made their living" so to speak. Ritualized practices were the means of maintaining the Cult of Sacrifice.

Many people think that very few cultures actually engaged in ritual human sacrifice. In fact, the practice took many forms throughout pre-history and was practiced in almost every culture of the past. Those forms we read about from ancient Egypt and ancient Greece were some of the most brutal forms of sacrifice that had been practiced for centuries before as archaeology has borne witness. The only changes men saw throughout pre-history were the various different forms of sacrifice, some more brutal than others, with different sacrificial objects to accomplish different results. Religious reformation was slow but sometimes it was more deadly and at other times more benign. Eventually, many cultures were told that the gods no longer interfered in the affairs of men. It was no longer necessary to fear catastrophe at their hands. Brutal deadly sacrifice was slowly replaced by animal and money sacrifice. The gods became fatherly and motherly figures teaching love, knowledge and piety. Still the means of control were ritual reenactments of the lives of the gods that became morality. The Cult of Sacrifice has always been alive and well.

We obtain a hint at how religious reformations came about if we look at how the reformation of Greek myths slowly evolved into secular philosophy. Early Greeks began to question the premises of their brutal religious practices by inventing some key questions about the nature of the universe. These questions challenged the view of the gods as brutal masters who demanded human sacrifice. The Greeks asked such questions as what is the relationship between the one and the many. What principles create change? Is it the spirits or earth-bound processes such as air, water, fire and earth? What is the role of the individual as an autonomous thinker and what of the collectives that demanded various forms of human sacrifice? As they grappled with these questions, their society developed along two tracks, one religious demanding ritual sacrifice and another secular demanding that the individual mind be allowed to question and investigate without the influence of religion. To a great extent, Ancient Greece was very much like our society in that both societies experimented with various forms of social structure and investigated such issues as a separation of church and state, the role of the individual in solving his own problems and the role of government in the lives of individuals.

If you examine the writings of Greek philosophers, you see the tension between secular analysis and religious dominance. Their example reminds us of the many intellectuals during our Enlightenment period that experienced a similar tension as they strove to understand the difference between a free mind and one enslaved by doctrine. During this period, a new vision once again strove to remove men from the slavery of the mind. This conflict continues to influence us today as we question the viability of sacrificing the individual to the demands of the state. We ask whether it is society or religion to which we should sacrifice our minds, our time, our possessions; and some of us ask whether there should be any sacrificing at all. Some of us think that the legacy of the Enlightenment, what thinkers like Locke and others struggled to understand was the issue of freedom versus tyranny. Should society defend and protect the human mind seeking to understand, prosper and flourish or should it be the instrument of enforcing sacrifice? This is the Founding Fathers versus the progressives.

Through the influence of the progressives today, the residue of the demand for human sacrifice looms as a deep threat. According to the progressives, it is immoral to be for "yourself" and moral to think of the whole. It is immoral to seek profit and moral to sacrifice for the good of the group. Indeed, the statement by President Obama quoted above was nothing more than an echo of the ideas that confounded the Greeks so many centuries ago and still confound us today. The Cult of Sacrifice was alive among the President's allies in the "Occupy Wall Street" pseudo-movement, while others, the true historical radicals in the New Capitalist Radicals, cried out for capitalism, freedom and individual rights.

Some would say that connecting ancient human sacrifice to modern calls for altruism is unfair. Yet, one of the most ancient examples of the tension between the one and the many has come down to us today in the form of Greek tragedy, a ritualized recreation of the lives of the gods and demigods. These plays helped people experience catharsis by seeing for themselves, as we see today on television and in the theater, how the gods lived and how they acted. Greek plays were virtual examples, morality plays if you will, on how ancient Greek citizens were supposed to live their lives.

You can observe two basic themes in Greek plays that you can also observe today in American theater and movies. These themes make up the "natural resources" so to speak of both Greek and American story telling. They are the "suffering savior" and "the battle of the sexes". These themes are repeated constantly in our stories today as they were in the plays of Greek tragedy. Each theme represented an ancient religious perspective; primitive forms of religion, so to speak, that laid the foundation for modern religion and political theory today.

Stories of Prometheus, Atlas, Hercules, Theseus, Odysseus, Oedipus, Perseus and more provided for the Greeks the examples that taught them how a creature like man, all too human and frivolous, could participate in world consuming events, suffer, struggle and fight against the gods and nature, take on tremendous challenges and defeat violent enemies, sometimes to die (sacrifice himself) as an offering or scapegoat for the good of the earth or the people.

Likewise, today, actors such as Tom Cruise, Bruce Willis and others play heroes who suffer and die to save the planet, America and little children. They participate in world consuming events, suffer, struggle and fight against the odds and nature, take on tremendous challenges and defeat violent enemies, sometimes to die (sacrifice themselves) as an offering or scapegoat for the good of the earth or the people. The images of these sacrificial offerings, these virtuous men, are intended to elicit admiration and a desire to live as they lived, to experience the "magnificence" of life as a successful sacrifice. These tragedies are the symbols of the Cult of Sacrifice.

These stories, both ancient Greek and contemporary American, are derived from earlier rituals and myths of pre-history where men were called upon to give up their lives, their children and their possessions for the sake of setting the world right. They represent the constantly repeating themes of the Cult of Sacrifice, the idea that was more than a mere suggestion but a demand for sacrifice made upon all men, of all parts of the world and for all time.

The Cult of Sacrifice has gone through many reformations

throughout history. As the Enlightenment began taking shape, many philosophers realized that religion had come under attack because of the new focus on reason inaugurated by the Enlightenment. Men began seeing that life could be "lived", enjoyed and that reason was the means of that enjoyment. Men began to question the religious life of self-sacrifice, humility and self-denial and liberated themselves from the shackles of religious intolerance. As some have observed, Ayn Rand for one, the backlash against the ideas of the Enlightenment took the shape of a "new" morality invented by Kant, but based upon the dusty old skeletons of the past, the Cult of Sacrifice. Kant's goal was to save religion from the Enlightenment and he did it by elevating "duty" as man's prime motivation, turning it into an "imperative" built into the structure of the mind. Through this "new" morality, we have the effort of the Cult of Sacrifice to throw off the dust of the past and redeem itself by once again controlling man's mind and actions. When Comte began to elaborate upon the principles of "altruism", otherism, the victory of Kant was sealed and the Enlightenment was killed. The Founding Fathers never had a chance.

Yet, the Enlightenment left us one legacy; the Constitution of the United States that defined liberty and rights for man. This document rescued one nation from the Cult of Sacrifice and provided, for a couple of hundred years, an example of the magnificence possible to a nation built on reason. For the next few centuries the struggle was between a new morality of freedom and the reconstituted but still dusty Cult of Sacrifice now championed by Kant, the pragmatists and evangelicals. Because the thinkers that ruled the universities were essentially Kantians and their descendants, the victory of the Cult of Sacrifice is near complete. During his terms, the President could say, as if it is a foregone conclusion, that he would not accept a bill (that is supposed to solve our problems) unless there is some sacrifice in the bill. In fact, because of the resurgence of the Cult of Sacrifice, you cannot be considered a good person unless you convince people that you are a pious practitioner of duty, altruism and "love". The suffering savior is back on the ash.

Let's look back to the past again so we can identify the one fact that centuries of world leaders, witch doctors, kings, queens and prime ministers have missed. With every demand of sacrifice that has been made, there has always been a presumption that something good would happen; earthquakes would be mild, the gods would be fed and appeased, the world would be set right. Just as our President promises a prosperous economy if there is more sacrifice, men have always been promised that each and every sacrifice will save men, quiet the seas, bring good fortune and generally make things better. When the feared consequences did not come, the sacrifice was considered to have worked. The rulers were pleased at their accuracy and demanded more loot. When the feared consequences came anyway, the rulers told men that they had not sacrificed enough, that next time they would need to sacrifice more people, more goats and chickens and more money. They demanded more blood and loot. There is never enough sacrificing.

What did we miss through all these centuries of sacrificing? There was seldom a thought that the dreaded catastrophes had nothing to do with whether men sacrificed or not; that no matter what men did or gave up, the consequence that eventually came, good or bad, would have come anyway. The sacrificing was irrelevant, a brutal, sad waste of human energy and love. It was sacrifice for the sake of sacrificing...as was the call for sacrifice by the President. It should be done, he said, because it was "the right thing to do".

It also did not occur to many men in the past to question the rulers who proclaimed themselves proficient at knowing what the gods wanted from men. They did not notice that the demand for sacrifice kept the rulers alive while they, the pious ones, lost their loved ones, even their goats and chickens not to mention their passion for life. And it did not occur to us that President Obama was seeking sacrifice, not because he knew it would solve our problems, but because he knew it would not solve our problems. President Obama was a high priest of the Cult of Sacrifice doing what other high priests before him had done: he was faking a moral superiority and making it possible for himself and his cronies to loot the substance of society.

The Cult of Sacrifice has never solved our problems and perhaps it is time to stop the sacrificing, recognize that the thinkers of the Enlightenment were on the right track. We should complete their work and profess again the idea that men do have rights and that the first purpose of government should be to prevent sacrifice, to protect the lives and property of the people.

If we want to solve our problems as a nation, we should look at the practitioners of the Cult of Sacrifice and "throw them all out".

Non-ideology

The next big mistake of the administration is one they inherited from pragmatism. It is also a mistake made by the entire country over many decades. This is the mistake of being non-ideological.

In the previous chapter, I hinted at this mistake when I wrote:

"Bailouts are an ideologically-based idea that has been stripped of its ideological context by intellectuals in order to mainstream the idea that they are merely rational thought. This intellectual mind trick has a sinister influence on a society of people who do not realize that bailouts are essentially fascist/socialist in nature. They are a piece of the puzzle that represents an effort to fool people into accepting dictatorship. If you accept bailouts, you can accept more bailouts. And you must also accept the way things are done by government. You must accept political bribes, graft and unconstitutional acts. You must accept the immoral as moral and you must learn to think of everything in reverse. When you hear a lie, it is social truth. When you tell the truth it is a capitalist lie. When you accept higher taxes, you are engaging in order to solve problems. When you cannot afford to live, it is Justice. But don't worry; our vital industries will continue to function and provide us with what we need. Our sacrifice will save us. That we can't afford a car that does not work very well is an indication that our government is forcing us to be socially responsible (That is a lie too)."

To understand how a "stripped down" ideology affects people, consider the anti-business philosophy that the President preaches. It is the philosophy that declares businesspeople are thieves and that doing business is a zero-sum game where every purchase is a loss to the buyer. Because of this view, many people believe that businesspeople are evil. And, without ever seeing a verified instance of this thievery in their lives, they vote for any politician who claims he will protect them against greedy businesspeople. The idea is a myth straight out of the ideology fostered by Karl Marx. The President used the same idea without its Marxist context and even declared that he was not anti-business. And here is the switch; a progressive can declare that he is non-ideological by keeping his Marxist ideology hidden. This is an effort to make Marxist/collectivist/re-distributive views appear to be merely objective rather than expressions of a dangerously deadly ideology. This is how people are fooled into voting for progressives, and today's progressives, the nastiest ever, are not only fooling you, they are deliberately trying to destroy you...unless you wake up.

In fact, those who fall for this bait and switch have fooled themselves because they have never looked outside the movies for any real indication that businesspeople are thieves. The result is that businesspeople keep providing them with products that improve their lives while their customers, seeking the best products, are still unappreciative of the exacting kind of morality required to make those products.

This anti-ideology ideology that consists of declaring a Marxist premise, without referring to the Marxist context, enabled the President to put into power people who could do virtually anything they wanted including lie, steal, probably even kill in the name of service to the United States of America.

In order to convince you that non-ideology is a mistake and that I'm not just expressing an arbitrary position because I don't like the President, I'd like to point out that all political statements and acts take place within a wider ideological context. Every act indicates the ideology that gives it life and whose premises argue for it. And, conversely, ideologies can only be defined according to their fundamental characteristics that are expressed by political acts and speech.

There are only two basic types of ideology. These are coercive ideologies (force) and liberty-based ideologies (freedom). Because force and freedom are fundamental opposites when it comes to political systems, any political act must be either force or non-force; meaning coercive or non-coercive. The two political opposites, the two opposing political ideologies are slavery versus freedom or force versus freedom.

A coercive ideology is defined by its operative principle, which is that the government has the right and the responsibility to rule or force people to act in ways that the government deems necessary. These coercive systems, as history has shown, are primarily monarchism, fascism, socialism and communism.

Why is it important to define an ideology according to its operative fundamental principle? The operative fundamental provides a powerful argument for the basic moral principles that each system requires. If you know the operative fundamental principle of a system, you can save yourself lots of time determining whether the system is good or evil. By knowing what such a system requires on a fundamental level, ideologically, you will be able to judge the words and actions of politicians and accept or reject them on that basis alone.

For instance, during the war years of the last century, we knew we were fighting against an enemy that was evil. Fascism exposed itself as amenable to collectivism which included racism and complete dominance by the government over the entire society. For this reason, most Americans rejected fascism, not merely because of its racism but because it was coercive and rights-violating; it was totalitarian. Yet, the morality that the Germans practiced, altruism, saw fascism as a better and more efficient system of government. They felt that society needed a dominant leader who could act without the restrictions of a parliamentary system. That leader, necessarily, had to have the right of summary judgment; the right to command and kill as he deemed necessary...without restriction. Once we identified that Hitler's system was coercive, we could fight it without doubting our resolve.

The three key characteristics of fascism are: collectivism, sacrifice and coercion. Socialism's key characteristics are the same as fascism except that socialism seeks to implement government control of vital industries so that free individuals do not accumulate too much wealth. Socialism adds a stronger anti-capitalist component (although fascism is also anti-capitalist), and in many respects is not too different from fascism. Once again we see that the vital characteristic of socialism is also coercive government. Communism is at the extreme range wherein government controls all aspects and all industries and again is based upon coercive powers. Of course, monarchy is unlimited rule by a king who has the role of moral authority, usually through religion, and is considered the voice of God on earth. Once again, the king's key power is the ability to command and kill at will. It is coercive.

Consider that the ideologies, the philosophical defenses for fascism, socialism and communism are the same. In order for society to operate efficiently, the argument goes; the government must have coercive powers. Yet, each system is fraught with corruption. In fact, corruption is a key characteristic of each of these systems as history has shown.

Political System	Social System	Dominant Morality	Use of Force
Fascism	Collectivism	Sacrifice	One man engaged in government coercion to control the use and management of private property
Socialism	Collectivism	Sacrifice	Government coercion to nationalize, own and manage vital industries and re-distribute income
Communism	Collectivism	Sacrifice	Total government control of all aspects of society
Monarchy	Collectivism / Nationalism	Sacrifice	Total control by the king
Representative Republican or limited government	Individualism	Self-interest	Limited government restricted to protecting individual and property rights

If Americans knew the ideological rules that govern the way they think as it relates to political systems, they would be able to judge the pronouncements of politicians and decide whether any of them have a hidden coercive agenda. They can't hide coercion; it is implicit in their statements. And since we live, for the most part, in a representative republic, we can vote these people out.

Needless to say, the words of the President, the call to sacrifice, his anti-business rhetoric, his demands for new regulations, class warfare, racial divisions and his overt crony capitalism, exposed the fact that he favored fascism. If we know that fascism, in terms of fundamentals, is the selective use of force by government against citizens, then we know that fascism was the President's ideological principle. Though he claimed to be offering rational solutions to the nation's problems, he was in fact, offering us fascism. His collectivism explains his class and racial warfare. His morality of sacrifice explains his policies of re-distribution, crony capitalism, bailouts, stimulus programs and various other political "solutions". This is, by definition, and in fact, fascism. He advocated coercion against citizens.

There is nothing rational about fascism. Yet Americans were duped by the fact that the President did not honestly represent the ideology behind his policies, actions and solutions. Were he to have argued openly for fascism, we would surely have rejected him. That is how he got away with fooling people.

Let's continue the analysis. If coercion, and the ability to use force in an unlimited way, characterizes fascism, socialism and communism, then the opposite principle must characterize any system that is non-coercive. Although there have been few examples of non-coercive systems, the best example is that of the United States of America. As is known, the founders did an exhaustive analysis of political systems throughout history and, in their efforts to eliminate or control all potentially coercive elements in government, they created a representative system that limited and restricted the government's ability to coerce and they sought to put into place certain measures that would make it difficult for a group of people to take over the government and turn it into a dictatorship within their lifetimes. These included separation of powers, checks and balances, limited powers and a constitution that specifically defined what a government could not do.

A major principle of our government was the placement of Congress as the body closest to the people. The House of Representatives is made up of a group of people each beholden to his or her constituents' freedoms and interests. The result was a liberty-based society where people were free to do as they decided without the fear of being manipulated by other parties. This system removed the anti-capitalist component found in dictatorship because it realized that people seeking to survive would create the best products to trade with others. This liberated self-interest, made possible capital accumulation (because they realized that capital accumulation was good), made possible free trade (because they realized that zero-sum trades were the exception not the rule) and established property rights that the government could not violate (because they realized that liberty and property rights are central to civilization).

Today, if you analyze our present system, you will see that in many ways we are a representative republic that is drifting toward fascism at an alarming rate. This fact is what created the Tea Party; but the real question is how did we get here? I think the answer is found in our philosophical drift away from ideology. The problem is non-ideology, the inability of people to define and translate into ideological terms, what our politicians are not telling us. We have allowed them to hide their true ideological goals. We are being educated to judge them according to the _intentions_ of their actions but not according to their _methods_ (coercion). If we do not correct our thinking, their methods will lead to the opposite of their so-called intentions. This is why bailouts don't work, why stimulus doesn't work, why re-distribution doesn't work: they are coercive in nature and they will not accomplish their intentions. It is time we let our representative government know they must change course and stop moving us down the road of fascism.

I think the cause of this intellectual drift away from ideology was the progressive movement. It might surprise you that this movement during its genesis was essentially fascist in nature. Many early progressives, including both Roosevelts, admired fascism tremendously and saw it as a very valuable tool for national leaders to get more done. This was the same period during which the Nazis and other fascist regimes began to grow. In fact, many American intellectuals saw Hitler's ability to control the economy and build massive highway systems and factories and armaments as an indication that fascism was a very practical idea, a good way for the government to improve the economy. They saw monetary inflation as Keynes saw it; as a way to create prosperity. They saw regulation as a way to manipulate the various parts of the economy to ensure stability. In short, they saw fascism as practical.

In fact, during the period when the progressive left grew up, the later part of the 19th century and early 20th century, we saw the ascendency of politicians who "knew how to get things done". Men such as Herbert Hoover were powerful organizers and technocrats who were thought of as smart, efficient and certain of their course. They were young, brash and commanding. They could control events through a powerful will to lead...like Hitler and Mussolini in a sense. Fascism and socialism were both considered effective ways for government to manage economies; they were a wave of the future and ideas whose time had come.

Progressive intellectuals bemoaned the fact that they had to deal with parliamentary restrictions on what they could do. They wanted progress and resented having to get approval from large bodies of government staffed by rich old men. They hated restrictions against interfering in the workings of the free market and they considered the Constitution to be a vestige of the past, no longer relevant because they, the progressives, had found better ways to get things done; not by leaving the people alone but by intelligently managing them, educating them and ensuring that they had the spirit of collective sacrifice and the social contract. To deal with Constitutional restrictions, they floated trial balloons to see if they would pass and they propagandized (told lies) against capitalism. They helped to create anti-trust that broke up big businesses and they vilified business tycoons in the press in order to create anti-capitalist prejudice among the people and justify the looting practices that they, not the tycoons, had in mind. They even encouraged union agitation, riots and work strikes against the tycoons in order to further vilify them and capitalism.

Many of them believed their own propaganda and thought of people as weak and unenlightened, amenable to manipulation by their betters. At the same time, they bemoaned the pedestrian-level intelligence of the masses while at the same time knowing that they must change the selfish brutes into more docile servants of the whole. They praised sacrifice and they created straw men out of conservatives while spewing an incessant anti-capitalist and anti-American global perspective. Their first big success in 1908 was the institution of the income tax. At first, the people thought they were just taxing the richest among them who had enough to fund the massive programs. They could only watch as their own taxes began to rise as well. Later, in 1935, the Social Security Act added another nail in the coffin for freedom. Other successes came with the application of Antitrust Laws in 1914 (originally passed by Republicans) that helped them break up large trusts and gave the politicians virtual control over the economy. Lots of protestations about the "public good" and helping the poor and other such propaganda enabled them to slowly advance their fascist and socialist agendas but without mentioning their ideology. That they were socialists, communists and fascists was not part of the discussion.

They were not the first to do this, however. The Fabian society in Britain was successful in fostering "socialist" programs piecemeal by asking for minor concessions from conservatives. This helped them set the basic principle of government coercion which, once established, created the slippery slope that would eventually lead, in America, to Roosevelt's New Deal and ObamaCare. The Fabians sold their programs as necessary to solve the inequities of capitalism and to help the poor. By shedding ideological labels and masquerading as "mainstream" politicians, the Fabians were able to advance socialist ideas without calling them socialist. Instead, they were deemed "practical" solutions to the problem of industrialization and capitalism. The public took such minor steps as "progressive" and thought that the Fabians had the right idea, to add some safeguards to society that would mitigate the harm done to people by acquisitive capitalists. Through small coercive measures, that had little impact in the "macroeconomic sense", they were able to bring Britain, over time, into socialism. Progressives had struck gold when they realized that "non-ideological" ideology was working and that their goals could be met over time. After the second world war, this approach seemed even more necessary. The fascist governments that the progressives had admired before the war were now the losers and it was discovered that they were less than nice; they had, in fact, murdered millions and the labels, "fascism" and "socialism" were seen as the causes of the brutality. Their ideology had lost favor. So to accomplish their goals of political success, post-war progressives had to shed ideology all together and pretend to an adherence to freedom.

They did not change their ideologies however; they merely changed their labels and terminology. They still wanted to control the economy because, like the European fascists before them, they saw it as a practical way to get things done. So they advanced their ideas in "practical" terms, like the Fabians, pointing out problems caused by capitalism (by means of anti-capitalism) and then offering a mildly coercive solution that would be passed by Congress.

No one likes being deceived and the recognition by many Americans that the progressives are up to no good, in ideological terms, is creating a serious backlash. That the vilest of the communist radicals of the 1960s have managed to resurrect communism and fascism without informing the people, is not something sober thinking people will merely sit back and watch. Most people know, unlike the President, that socialism and fascism don't work and these clowns, the Soros types, the Ayers, the Sterns and the Rathkes are throwbacks to a time of violent revolution that the "Silent Majority" rejected years ago.

Yet, here they are, pretending to be "practical" thinkers with "practical" solutions. Their Alynsky tactics are merely the same philosophies that characterized the other street fighter, Hitler. Some Americans know that the President and his supporters behind the scenes want slavery. And they are practical enough to avoid throwing out our semi-capitalist base and resist the progressives' efforts. The coming election (2016) may be our last chance to repudiate the ideologies of fascism and socialism. Good riddance. There are still some heaps of rubble along the highway near Munich where they can spend their retirements.

The problem with non-ideology is that people who are non-ideological are no longer able to connect, in practical terms, their political ideas with the actual decline taking place around them. As politicians clamor for more power, the decline of the economy, because of the anti-capitalism left over from the progressive era, continues unabated and forces them to blame all the problems of society on rich people and capitalism as did their forebears. That the decline of the economy has always been the result of progressive tinkering in the economy was a lesson we did not learn. It is the lesson about which Radical Capitalists are reminding people. Our past inability to say, "This is fascism, and because so, we must not go this way," leaves us in a position where progressives can declare, "Anyone who would call this fascism is an ignorant person who doesn't understand history." I say, "Balderdash." We call it fascism because that is what it is and we know it because we do understand both history and cause and effect.

We, those of us who advocate capitalism and limited government are the last standing adults in the room, so to speak. We have allowed the voices of non-ideology to imply that a wonderful future can be built by ignoring the ideological foundations of our ideas while knowing that those ideas are not practical and that they will not accomplish their stated utopia. We know it is a fool's errand. So we watch the events of the world, knowing full well that those engaged in leadership are destroying society.

During the Obama years, we knew that society was being led by people in the administration and the media who averted their eyes from the devastating consequences of our government's fascist policies. The President's call for more sacrifice, higher taxes, bigger government programs, bailouts, violations of the sanctity of contract and law, more government regulations and almost daily violations of the Constitution are aspects of fascism. Such measures always will be fascist in nature and the result will always be more suffering, fewer jobs, hunger, economic depression and poverty, possibly even death or prison for those of us who do not go along.

Certainly, *now*, we know that Hitler's fascism, his control of the German economy, did not work. Beneath his short-term success was monetary easing that resulted in inflation, corruption and demoralization of the people. With every day that inflation raged in Germany and with every day during the war, Germany became weaker economically and eventually lost the war. The preparation for war had been based on a lie and the seeming strength of Germany was nothing but image-building and propaganda. The Germans lost because fascism can never help a nation restore its pride; it can only destroy pride and turn the nation into a pariah which will eventually become a land of rubble.

It has been said, that German ideology made the people blind to the concentration camps in their midst. Like horses with blinders, the Germans saw only the forward march into oblivion and none of the devastation that they were building. Likewise, today, because of our non-ideology, some of us are unable to see that our concentration camps are being built by the daily cuts of fascist Executive Orders, fascist monetary easing and fascist inflation.

The Germans did not think that their sacrifice would cause their cities to be bombed and destroyed. Nor did they think that fascism always exploits the people until their energies are spent. They were taught to expect a bright and sun-filled future that never came. We, on the other hand, have time to stop the fascist disaster coming to us. But in order to stop it, we must recognize that the methods we are using to accomplish our "intentions" are fascist in nature and that they will sap our rights and energy until there is nothing left but rubble. Eventually, we'll weaken and the world will gladly destroy us to rid itself of our once noble ideology. They will blame our demise on freedom and then proceed to stumble after us into oblivion.

Reality versus Intentions

"One of the great mistakes is to judge policies and programs by their intentions rather than their results." - Milton Friedman

I've always thought the above quote was flawed. It seems to me that judging results in order to evaluate government programs is a false approach. All you get are lies, propaganda and glowing statistics from those who favor such programs. You'll never get into a substantive debate about the real issues such as the role of government and the role of liberty or even the nature of rights. You wind up with an endless debate about what works and what doesn't – which reduces the debate to a fruitless discussion of how much force should be exerted against citizens – not whether force should be allowed at all. This approach cedes the basic principle to the progressives and leaves the door open to more force in the long-run.

Yet, when I recently saw Professor Friedman's quote again on a Facebook post, it reminded me that he was also referring to a cognitive issue. There is a reason why progressives focus more on the intentions of their policies than on the results. Their overall intellectual level, their disdain for logic and clear reasoning, their inability to see cause and effect as well as their erroneous use of a presumed moral mandate have blinded them to reality. Like thugs, who do not deserve the power their government-issued guns afford, they have convinced themselves that their poorly conceived intentions are moral and this gives them the right to demand that men provide the funds to support them. This also gives them the right to be unconcerned about whether they achieve their intentions. It is simply unimportant to them.

The idea that "moral" intentions justify government force is flawed at base. To explain this, we must understand how people define the good in society. There are essentially three methods. The first is that the good is defined by God, the second, that it is defined by the collective and the third is that it is defined by the individual for himself.[14]

The first two approaches to the good have always presented problems for society. Firstly, both approaches have been imposed upon men by means of that moral mandate we mentioned, a social contract, the will of the people or brute force. Secondly, they are justified by fallible individuals who claim to be the voice of God or the voice of the people. Who can argue with God, the first

---

[14] "For centuries, the battle of morality was fought between those who claimed that your life belongs to God and those who claimed that it belongs to your neighbors—between those who preached that the good is self-sacrifice for the sake of ghosts in heaven and those who preached that the good is self-sacrifice for the sake of incompetents on earth. And no one came to say that your life belongs to you and that the good is to live it. "Both sides agreed that morality demands the surrender of your self-interest and of your mind, that the moral and the practical are opposites, that morality is not the province of reason, but the province of faith and force. Both sides agreed that no rational morality is possible, that there is no right or wrong in reason—that in reason there's no reason to be moral. "Whatever else they fought about, it was against man's mind that all your moralists have stood united. It was man's mind that all their schemes and systems were intended to despoil and destroy. Now choose to perish or to learn that the anti-mind is the anti-life." – Ayn Rand, Atlas Shrugged, This is John Galt Speaking

group asks, while the second group asks who can argue with the will of the people? Finally, these two views of the good don't provide a standard for what the good actually is. The first holds that the good is intrinsic, made right simply because God has deemed it while the second group holds that the good is whatever society decides. Both approaches subject society to the whims of men who do *not* have special knowledge. These two views are the sources of tyranny and the American Revolution was a rebellion against them.

The Founders of our society had a different view. They knew that each individual was sovereign and had the right to the pursuit of happiness. For them, this right was real, and neither men nor society should be allowed to violate it. This implied that the individual was responsible for deciding the good for himself according to his own standards. The implication of this view is that the individual should be free to use reason and apply it to his life. It held that he had the right to apply his best knowledge to any problem or, if he makes a mistake, to pursue and apply new knowledge that corrects the mistake.

Notice that in letting the individual decide the good for himself, we prohibit the other two views from being imposed upon man. This shows the moral power of self-sufficiency and how clearly the Founders knew that freedom was a moral issue. In addition, letting the individual decide for himself is the best way to ensure that most of the solutions men define will be based upon a correct ascertainment of reality and a clear connection between free will and success in life. This individualist view liberates people to be "reality-based"; realistic and constantly learning because no one has made the final decision for them to follow. It holds that life is a process of growth and improvement for those men who choose to think.

This is why capitalism[15] is such a successful system; it enables reason and leaves men free to judge reality based upon their own learning and knowledge rather than that of a government technocrat. What one man decides for himself will likely also be decided by other thinking men for themselves since all are focused on reality rather than ancient scripts and the dictates of Mao interpreting Marx.

I've noticed that many young people today do not realize that their freedom directly leads to their ability to make a profit. They are unaware that collectivism, the idea that the collective determines the good, destroys profit and the ability to flourish. The collectivist ideas that are taught to them in school destroy their ability to live according to their own thinking; to live by their own minds and this destroys their ability to compete and profit from their work. In fact, they have lost the knowledge of recent history that exposes the flaws of collectivism. That recent history was that of East and West Germany.

---

[15] "Capitalism is a social system based on the recognition of individual rights, including property rights, in which all property is privately owned." – Ayn Rand, "Capitalism, the Unknown Ideal", What is Capitalism?

The poverty of the communist east before Reagan was due to the fact that socialism/communism defined the "good" intentions for which people were forced to work. Many people who lived in East Germany remember how poor society had become and how demoralized people were that they could do nothing about it. I remember seeing filthy and poorly dressed East Germans visiting their relatives in the West; the contrast between them was palpable. It was easy to identify them; their dress, grooming, lack of self-confidence were clear signals that they had not been raised in the West. Their West German relatives, on the other hand, were prosperous, clean, well-groomed and self-confident. Their homes had new furniture and television sets and their towns were clean and well maintained. Later, while visiting East Berlin, I noticed the decrepit buildings, the often un-bathed people and their silent despair. Today, we are being asked to give up our freedoms in order to establish similar conditions in America.

East and West Germany were testaments to the power of ideas. People's lives were directly affected by whether they were asked to sacrifice for the collective or work toward their own well-being. The idea that the collective is all powerful, that it defines the good toward which people should work, stood in stark contrast to the idea that people should be free to think and determine their own destinies by means of their own thinking. West Germany was a country of tall buildings and vibrant affluence whose people enjoyed life; whereas East Germany was a country where the tallest buildings were the massive towers from which they were watched by their government, where technology was used to spy on people rather than improve their lives.

The actual cause of affluence in society is capitalism not re-distribution. In a capitalist system, productive citizens are allowed to keep their earnings and invest them as they see fit. The result is more jobs and more people earning enough money to buy an ever growing inventory of newly produced products. Capitalism reduces the poverty rolls because it creates jobs for people and turns people into producers (and consumers). Capitalism also raises standards of living and creates a "snowball" effect where the more capital that productive citizens accumulate, the better are the capital improvements in society. In other words, capital accumulation and the free flow of capital in a capitalist system mean better highways, better electricity grids, better manufacturing facilities, better homes, better jobs, better communication networks, etc., all of which affect the long-term comfort of people and the viability of society.

Imagine the surprise of the East Germans when they saw the large numbers of products and services that their West German relatives were routinely enjoying. What they felt was betrayal because they had been taught in school that the west was poor and collapsing. They realized that what they saw everywhere in the west could not be a mere show designed to fool them. They knew that the prosperity they saw was capitalism...many of them cried to have been so massively deceived.

Why was the difference between east and west so stark? Why did the same ideas of today's progressives cause the communist system to regress in such a way? Why was everything collapsing in the east and shooting up in the west? Why wasn't socialism able to create the improvements that capitalism put within the grasp of even the poorest citizens? The answer is clear: It is progressive policies and programs that destroy progress and bring people to poverty and decay. The progressives are really the "regressives."

To show that progressivism causes society to regress, we must remember what the progressives have always promised. We must remember their "intentions". Their main value to society, they claim, is that they are expanding freedoms for those who are supposedly left behind by capitalism. For instance, capitalism provides the freedom of upward mobility and secure jobs while the progressives promise to advance beyond these to welfare, unemployment insurance, higher wages and union protection (to name a few). Yet, the freedoms promised by progressives come at a price; they must be paid for by money taken from the producers, the factory owners, the wealthier and the middle class. Where the freedom offered by capitalist society is the freedom to act, the "freedom" offered by progressivism is the freedom not to act, paid for by those who act. Progressives promise to extend freedom but they do it by enslaving a part of society – those who are able to satisfy their own wants. Progressivism harms the best and most productive among us in order to extend invented "freedoms" to the less productive. This is not merely a new definition of freedom; it is a bait and switch.

Another example of regressive government policies is socialized medicine. A government program that is intended to increase the availability of medical care will actually decrease that availability and destroy medical care in the long run. By claiming a "right" to free medical care for the poor, the government is defining "social justice", while disregarding the rights of doctors and others in the medical industry. By interfering in the profits of medical industry professionals (who must make profits in order to stay in business), the government is turning these professionals into government employees beholden to the decisions of bureaucrats. On a minute-by-minute basis, all medical decisions are subordinated to a bureaucrat's view of "social responsibility" rather than giving the patient proper care. The overall result is a slave camp professing love for mankind. "Arbeit Macht Frei."

In a socialized medical system, the targets to be exploited are doctors, medical professionals and other private companies dedicated to providing products and cures. Doctors will be monitored and evaluated, ostensibly to root out fraud, so government can justify paying them less for their services. This reduces their profits and re-distributes them to people who get free care or drugs. The same would go for other medical professionals that government would unionize. Unionism would force the more productive nurses and specialists to work harder to prevent the less productive from harming or killing patients. Private industry organizations would face huge compliance standards and reporting requirements as well as provide free services and products, all of which reduce their profits and re-distributes their money to the bureaucrats and poor. The result is that none of the intended benefits of socialized medicine are realized.

Socialized medicine is actually a vast re-distribution scheme where the most talented and able are forced out of the system precisely because of their special knowledge and skills. By taking the profits out of medical care, the socialized system destroys those providing the best products and offering the most cures. The medical industry will have its profits wrung out of it by various reforms so that some patients can get their care for free. The result will be fewer doctors, fewer medical industry professionals and fewer companies competing for a dwindling medical dollar. The result will be lower quality care available to fewer people, long lines and stressed out medical workers who no longer enjoy their jobs, not to mention people who die while waiting for treatments.

Once again, the solution to providing better medical care to more people is capitalism. Capitalism enables capital accumulation (since there are no taxes) and this enables private research and development over long periods. The incentive of huge profits would drive the industry to produce better and less expensive cures over time.

Products or cures that work best find customers who are able to pay for them while production improvements and additional research bring the cost of the more expensive cures down over time. Eventually, what were once expensive cures are brought down within the budgets of more people. Private insurance that is truly free is able to help people bear the costs of highly expensive cures while patients responsible for their own health care pay out of pocket for more common sicknesses. As the health care "system" grows, more and more people live longer lives.

We could engage in this exercise for virtually every "intention" of the progressives and we will find that coercive, re-distributive measures actually slow progress and fail to realize the intended benefits. Every re-distribution program is a de facto transfer of money and, therefore, it is possible for someone somewhere to skim, either by being allowed to raise prices to exorbitant levels or by stealing. Payoffs, bribes, government "investments" and extortion become the order of the day. And the more massive the government program, the more massive is the money laundering it enables.

The idea that the collective determines the "good" in society is called collectivism. Collective unity is glorified as a panacea for all problems today and is considered by many to be a wonderful expression of group strength and survivability. In fact, President Obama often spoke about and glorified the collective spirit of our forebears as if collectivism, sacrifice for others, and not individualism, made America strong. This was a deliberate deception.

The President wanted to associate collective sacrifice with strength in America. If he could make sacrifice into the highest value of society, there will be no end to the sacrificing – and no end to the money laundering.

Collectivism is one of the evilest ideas in history. It is the cause of much of the evil that has been done on the planet. It is the refuge of the dictator and mass murderer who uses the idea to force people into herds of mindless slaves. Collectivism despoils society and life and it forces people to give up their minds and self-respect. It forces them to join a "unity" that demands self-sacrifice and destroys self-esteem. It makes everything dirty in society because it forces the individual to assume that someone else will do something to solve his problems and it relieves the beneficiary of the responsibility for his or her life. When nothing gets done, the leaders blame those of ability for not sacrificing enough. Collectivism always destroys the ablest and removes them from society, leaving a vacuum to be filled by the incompetents who had been complaining about never being given a fair chance.

When I say that collectivism makes everything dirty, I mean it literally. In my travels around the world, I've noticed that the more collectivist societies are always the dirtiest. I think this is because there is no practical (profit) motive that would move anyone to take responsibility for his area. Collectivist societies have "renters" not owners. Since no one owns anything, no one takes responsibility for maintenance and upkeep. No one sees a benefit to maintaining, cleaning and repairing anything because the government is supposed to see to it. But the government doesn't do it. Government officials, also do not own anything. They are responsible but no one is keeping track. The entire society gets older and dirtier while everyone waits for someone to do something. This extends even to peoples' homes and living environments. People refuse to care for themselves and their surroundings because they are always waiting for someone to take responsibility. From the welfare mother who raises numerous kids on the dole, to the high-bred executive who runs a bailed out enterprise, there is nothing to be done while waiting for the government to save them.

Contrast this to societies based on private property, where profit is possible and where there are no restrictions on the flow of capital. The owners of property know that their profits will increase if they maintain their areas. Shops are cleaner, brighter and more enjoyable to visit; restaurants are clean and they make tasty food so customers will come back. Janitors are everywhere mopping and sweeping. Capitalist society is always cleaner and more open. People are happier and more active. This is what the profit motive does to society.

Yet, we are told that the profit motive is evil. It creates a surplus that the rich spend on yachts and wild sex parties. Progressives tell us that such profits are actually stolen from the poor and should be recovered by the government on behalf of the people. Capitalism has failed, they tell us, and only the collective unity of socialism can correct its errors. Such arguments are the stuff of which massive, failed government programs are made.

The practice of using collectivism to justify theft and coercion makes it difficult for many people to recognize that corruption is gaining a foothold in society. Certainly, those committed to collective action think they are being nice when they ask people to sacrifice for the good of the whole; but they don't realize that the collective "system" gives people no choice about having their production confiscated. Certainly, progressives use magic words like "social justice" and "social contract" or they invoke the "will of the people" to justify what they are doing to the people, but the bottom line, so to speak, is coercion; someone must be forced to pay for it. You have no choice about it...regardless of how eloquent they are in telling you to sacrifice.

Another real-life example of failed collectivist policy was the government's effort to increase home ownership between the periods 1994 to 2010. Politicians told us that banks should be required to make money available to poor people who wanted to buy homes. In this case, the government used a bogus study that accused banks of redlining certain neighborhoods and denying mortgage loans to people who lived there. They pointed out that many of those neighborhoods were filled with black people and they accused the banks of racism. They insisted that banks aggressively issue mortgage loans to the poor – under threat of prosecution. And the government even knew of a group that could help recruit those new homeowners, namely ACORN. The result is that loans (dollars) which would have gone to credit-worthy customers were re-distributed to people with questionable payment histories. As I said, all re-distribution programs are money laundering schemes and the Community Reinvestment Act was the biggest money laundering scheme of all. Poor people were used so that corrupt government officials could transfer huge sums of money from the banks to the Democrats.

The government's collectivist policies, its interference in the mortgage industry, eventually led to the collapse of Fannie Mae and Freddie Mac, two quasi-governmental organizations responsible for purchasing the loans. Because of the massive numbers of risky loans, these organizations exerted a huge influence over the economy and especially over the financial services industry. Some government officials saw the danger to the economy. They realized that any downturn in the mortgage industry could seriously harm the entire economy. Some politicians (the "evil" John McCain and George W. Bush) attempted to rein in Fannie Mae and Freddie Mac but their efforts were re-buffed by mostly Democratic politicians who thought there were no problems with this system as long as housing prices continued to rise; and as long as no one raised any alarms.

During this period of home ownership expansion, it

appeared that socialism was working and that the Democrats had discovered a cash cow in the banks. All of the faulty loans were re-packaged into investment vehicles and given the backing of the Federal Government which spread the money laundering cancer to the financial services industry otherwise known as Wall Street. Yet, it was all temporary and illusory. With the glut of money available for home purchases and the aggressive lending facilitated by ACORN and the CRA, housing prices continued to rise until the financial system became flooded with the faulty loans. High oil prices in the summer of 2008 forced people to stop making their mortgage payments and the house of cards collapsed. This was good news for the Democrats who were responsible because they could now use the collapse as a weapon in the coming Presidential election. A panicked George W. Bush was boxed in. He and the Republicans were now being falsely blamed for the failure of capitalism. In an effort to save the election for the Republicans, he bought into a "solution" that meant even more money laundering. He proposed the Troubled Assets Relief Program (TARP) which created shivers of alarm among the American people. The entire fiasco gave Presidential candidate Obama an opportunity to criticize the Republicans for policies that even he supported as the lawyer who fought for the expansion of the CRA.

But the housing bubble and the collapse of the financial services industry were created solely by the government's forcing the banking industry to issue risky loans. The very people responsible for it were swept into power to give us more money laundering schemes such as massive stimulus programs (that stimulated nothing) and the Affordable Care Act (that would re-distribute medical services).

Program	Intention	Coercion Exerted	Result
Welfare	Provide support until the individual can support him or herself	Taxpayer dollars taken from productive citizens	More welfare and fewer jobs
Community Reinvestment Act	Provide homes for the less advantaged	Bank investments diverted from productive investments	Housing crash
Anti-trust	Breakup large trusts and increase competition	Government mandates to break up corporations or fine them	Less competition
Affordable Care Act	Provide medical coverage for every American	Individual Mandate	Death Panels, reduced services, long lines, fewer doctors, poor service, higher costs
Government Funded Education	Provide better education to students	Taxation, compulsory education, indoctrination	Social engineering, lower test scores, propaganda, poorly educated students
GM and Chrysler Bailouts	Save auto industry	Taxation	Green cars no one buys, cash for clunkers, reduced buying power of consumers, lower economic conditions, fewer jobs overall, prolong eventual collapse

Coercion against peaceful citizens is anti-mind and anti-life. It stifles the ability of people to take the necessary "free" action that would solve their problems. For instance, a government official, with large amounts of taxpayer dollars, could never establish the first electrical grid. This is because the activity of inventing an electrical grid can only be engaged in by free people (with certain skills) seeking to make a profit.

In capitalism, great enterprises are possible because real solutions for real problems can only be found by free minds capable of invention. Capitalism requires reason, the creation of values, free choice, free trade, capital accumulation and the free flow of capital. Capitalism is the only system where the "intentions" of individuals can be tied to their self-interest and especially to the quality of their thinking. Capitalism does not impose intentions that people should be forced to pursue; it lets people define their own intentions and it gives them the freedom to achieve them and to profit.

Every program advanced by progressives restricts the free flow of capital and expropriates money from the productive sector in some way. This means that it does harm to the workings of the capitalist system; it restricts "reason, the creation of values, free choice, free trade, capital accumulation and the free flow of capital". Each instance of expropriation drains a part of the productive economy; taking the money and energy of productive citizens and putting them to less productive use or totally wasting them. Each government program takes away a piece of the product of society and eats the substance of society in some way. The intentions of those programs are never accomplished.

I mentioned earlier that progressives have a disdain for reason which makes them incapable of converting their intentions into practical results. One example of this is the idea that government can stimulate an economy by giving consumers more money. But the money that would stimulate demand is already in the economy. It is being removed from one group of people, the producers, who are already spending it in the economy and giving to another group of people who will spend it. There is no new demand being created.

Yet, progressives continue to impose their intentions on society. Sometimes they want to re-distribute money. At other times, they'll re-distribute skills and intelligence, and at other times human energy. Their methods are varied, but the key to the essence of progressivism is coercion. Some programs only "steal" a small amount of money and their economic impact is lost to our immediate vision. But the cumulative effect of millions of small thefts will eventually eat at society and bring us to a tipping point where the "interest" is gone, where the profits have been taken away and where there is no reason left to produce. At this point, we return to the jungle and fade away as a nation.

The fading away of America is coming and the only way to stop it is to end the massive government programs so people can start living again. Whether ending these programs is done slowly or immediately, it must be done if we are to survive. But once it is done, all those intentions that are now forced upon us by progressives will become the intentions of real living innovators who will find a way to accomplish them while making a profit. Once profit is put back into human transactions, America, the nation destroyed by progressives, will return.

There is no way to stop the juggernaut of progressivism in society without repudiating it totally and insisting that we be allowed to be self-interested – which means that we be free to use reason, free to make the right decisions and free to profit from them. Don't let the progressives make you feel guilty for wanting to live – celebrate your right to the fruit of your labor and the fruit of your mind. Celebrate your right to enjoy your life without government expropriation. Celebrate your love of values and tell anyone who demands sacrifice to go straight to Hell.

Without the repudiation of progressive intentions, we are doomed to living on a planet of wars, self-destruction and moral guilt not to mention poverty and disease. Changing the culture and liberating minds requires a philosophical argument against altruism and self-sacrifice. Altruism has become so engrained on the planet that it is everywhere, implicit and taken for granted. Only a conscious, philosophical approach can defeat it. It cannot be done today or by the time of the election. It will take years; but the struggle must begin and the challenges must be verbalized.

So if you want to stop the progressive juggernaut, you

have to say to the progressives, by any means at your disposal, "You are stealing and it is time to stop." You can say it through blogs, articles, videos, discussion groups and by voting. You must tell people that altruism is not a benevolent idea and, as a nation, we must begin the process of challenging its power and its hold on the minds of millions. Short of this, the inexorable power of ideas will carry our nation further into decline. As long as altruism goes unchallenged, there is no stopping its deadly influence. There is no stopping the progressives.

Compare the approach to progress taken by the Framers of the Constitution. Their intent was not to foster a particular intention out of context and force individuals to accomplish it. Instead, their approach was much more sophisticated. They understood the broad sweep of values and liberties necessary for individual accomplishment. They saw the value of establishing the type of society that protected individual rights and enabled people to thrive and flourish. They knew that freedom enabled moral living.

The Founders' intention was not to *provide* for people but to *liberate* people so they could provide for themselves. This revolution in political thinking made our nation the most moral in history. It elevated the individual to the level of sovereignty over his own life and removed all obstacles to his pursuit of the good. It enabled pride rather than guilt and force.

Today, with massive re-distribution and money laundering

taking place, progressivism has shown itself to be bereft of ideas and solutions. It continues to wallow in the intellectual decay created by Marxism and fascism, offering the same tired lies and methods that were used by Stalin, Mao and Pol Pot. The "solutions" it offers are the weapons of force that kept man in tatters and hunger for centuries.

There is nothing in the ideas of today's left toward which people should move. A good example of the bankruptcy of the left is the atrocious Affordable Care Act. This bill is a labyrinth of Marxist-style re-distribution schemes so complex that people are not supposed to notice that it is actually a man-made abyss where money just disappears. The bill has so many coercive elements, each working to re-distribute money, time and skills, in so many ways that it is mind-boggling. It demands that people accept corruption as "normal", as the way things are done, as the new "moral", to such a degree, that what people end up accepting is pure evil. Lurking beneath the words that promise health care is the cynical use of a once great medical care system to dispense death.

I know people who claimed to feel violated when the Supreme Court ruled that the ACA was constitutional. This act is an affront to the dignity and self-respect that previously free people had always felt in the past. Its corruption changes society drastically and spreads a pall of uncleanliness everywhere. It is as if collectivism has taken the soul out of people and forced them to think, what should I do, how do I accommodate the new demands being made upon me? How do I deal psychologically with the prying hands of society as it has its way with my body, with my health and with my future?

The progressives of today don't realize that today's negative news and economic numbers are caused by their own coercive policies; and because they can't believe that their ideas are creating today's problems, they double down on the talking points; and, finally, rather than desist from advancing their disastrous policies, they insist on making things worse.

The progressives have become automatons who wonder what's wrong with the world, totally oblivious to the fact that what *is* wrong with the world is progressivism.

Standing My Ground

The next big mistake of the Obama administration was the encouragement of race divisions, violence and race wars.

When one of the President's favorite communists, Van Jones, essentially called all conservatives racists, he betrayed a common method of deception that has been engaged by totalitarians for many decades.[16] It is the method of using collective thinking (group thinking) when discussing the actions of individuals. A crime is not a group phenomenon; it is engaged in by an individual seeking to harm another individual. It is a volitional act and is therefore the responsibility of the individual who perpetrated the harm. Properly, crime legislation should be about protecting the individual rights of the victim, not about any sort of bogus group rights. Groups don't have rights; only individuals do. When individual issues are dealt with according to group conflicts, such thinking poisons the minds of people and the results are prejudice and unfair treatment toward individuals.

Some of you will remember Van Jones as the one-time Obama Czar responsible for transitioning our industrial economy from fossil fuels to green energy. This initiative was part of a grand strategy that combined Cap and Trade

---

[16] *"...listen, you've got the perfect storm building. You've got all the passion around Trayvon, and what a horrible injustice that was. And it turns out you can draw a direct line back to the Koch Bros, you can draw a direct line back to mainstream corporations..."*

legislation and global warming fears with government investments in green technologies.

Let's leave aside the issue that this initiative could not possibly have succeeded for a variety of reasons. Let's stay on Van Jones. You will recall that, once it was discovered that Mr. Jones was an avowed Marxist, several individuals on the "right" began to expose past statements made by Mr. Jones that did not represent "mainstream" ideas. A clarion call went out that the President was promoting, without the advice and consent of the Senate, communists and other radicals who were decidedly anti-American. Soon, very soon, Mr. Jones was fired and put out to pasture.

Or so we thought. I had a suspicion at the time that the radical left did not want Mr. Jones to disappear. In fact, since he was famously fired, Mr. Jones was everywhere. His statement that he was no longer a communist was incongruous to say the least. His claim that he wanted to hire unemployed youth in government subsidized "green" companies was a farce. His work to indoctrinate children with communist principles was certainly dubious, and his posing as a thinker with new ideas (really old Marxist ideas) on how to make industry more socially responsible should also have been questioned.

For a while, I thought we were viewing an orchestrated effort to make this man look like a capitalist with lots of conservative ideas. I got the impressions that his supporters wanted us to let our guard down and let him once again return to the family of man. Instead, Mr. Jones eventually burst out of his shell and revealed himself again for what he truly was: a partisan propagandist for class and race warfare. He shed his temporarily acquired "pro-capitalist" persona in order to tell us that all of white American society is racist. He found his new truth in the Trayvon Martin scandal and especially in the "stand your ground" laws. These laws, he declared, were an effort to kill innocent blacks on the streets.

What Mr. Jones ignored was that the "stand your ground" law in Florida also applied to and protected black people. But let's stay on track. What he seemed to be saying is that the Koch Brothers (two influential conservative businesspeople who support Republican causes), through an organization known as ALEC[17], has funded a legislative effort to establish "stand your ground" laws in 22 states. To date, this supposedly "racist" law is in place in Florida, the state in which Trayvon Martin was killed. So the thinking goes: Trayvon Martin is black. He was killed because of the "stand your ground" law. In other words, the "white racist" George Zimmerman killed him because he was free to stand his ground against blacks who attack whites. This makes the "stand your ground" law racist, and since its implementation was supported by ALEC which is supported, in part, by the Koch Brothers, this makes the Koch Brothers racists and this makes Florida a racist state and ALEC which is an organization dedicated to conservative issues, is also racist. Because

---

[17] American Legislative Exchange Council

conservatives are mostly white, then all white conservatives are racists, and, well, let's be consistent, all whites are racist by nature (Critical Race Theory). I think that pretty well says the unsaid here, except for one more conclusion: since ALEC supports conservative causes and the group most often opposes progressive causes, being against progressivism is also racist. This means all whites and all conservatives are racists and so they should all be put in jail because they are white. I'm not sure if it also means all white progressives are racists too. I think it depends on whether they vote for President Obama.

Needless to say, this "revelation" by Van Jones of just how racist conservatives are would have been important information for voters in the lead up to the 2012 election. Everyone must get on the bandwagon and totally repudiate all conservatives and Republicans. Not just Coke and Pepsi (which I will never purchase again), but everybody should do everything they can to expose ALEC and ensure that this crony-capitalist scheme (as described by progressives) is put out of business and boycotted especially on election day. That means voting overwhelmingly for the only honest politician who is working for the middle class against corporate America, you know the guy from Chicago whose cause is so righteous that he only helps corporations that bundle money for his election, yes, Barack Obama, the union money launderer who is the favorite candidate of Mickey Mouse.

Of course, I'm speaking facetiously but not any more facetious than the idea that all whites are racists. So, let's get back to reality. The concept of "stand your ground" is not new. In fact, courts have considered the issue in several cases as far back as 1906 and generally, they have sided with the person being violently attacked. It has never been considered an issue that enabled racist whites to kill innocent blacks...at least not until now. Wikipedia describes "stand your ground" this way:

"A stand-your-ground law states that a person may use force in self-defense when there is reasonable belief of a threat, without an obligation to retreat first. In some cases, a person may use deadly force in public areas without a duty to retreat. Under these legal concepts, a person is justified in using deadly force in certain situations and the "stand your ground" law would be a defense or immunity to criminal charges and civil suit. The difference between immunity and a defense is that an immunity bars suit, charges, detention and arrest. A defense permits a plaintiff or the state to seek civil damages or a criminal conviction. More than half of the states in the United States have adopted the Castle doctrine, stating that a person has no duty to retreat when their home is attacked. Some states go a step further, removing the duty of retreat from any location. "Stand your Ground", "Line in The Sand" or "No Duty to Retreat" laws thus state that a person has no duty or other requirement to abandon a place in which he has a right to be, or to give up ground to an assailant. Under such laws, there is no duty to retreat from anywhere the defender may legally be. Other restrictions may still exist; when in public, a person must be carrying the firearm in a legal manner, whether concealed or openly".[18]

What this means is that "stand your ground" legislation is not some recently cooked up racist idea from some Republican smoke-filled room. It is not intended to suppress the black vote or commit genocide against the entire black race. "Stand your ground" is a principle that has nothing to do with race, has had a long history of case law and is really about immunizing the individual against frivolous law suits when he happens to survive and win out over a criminal who was intent on robbing or killing him.

In view of this long history of "stand your ground" legislation, consider what Van Jones is saying. The whole history of the "Stand your ground" legal battle is a right wing racist conspiracy that goes back to 1906. The fact (if it is a fact) that the Koch Brothers are behind recent efforts to extend "stand your ground" legislation is considered by Mr. Jones as proof that they have a racist intent to kill blacks "at will". Is Mr. Jones aware of the extensive case law about this concept? Does he understand that in the past even progressive Supreme Court Justices have defended the principle of "stand your ground"? Is he aware that "stand your ground" is actually a response to past laws that demanded a retreat before a person could defend himself? I would say that these facts

---

[18] http://en.wikipedia.org/wiki/Stand-your-ground_law

are irrelevant to Mr. Jones because they do not justify the conclusion that he wants to draw, that the Koch Brothers are racists and that white society wants to kill black people.

I question the intent of Mr. Jones's effort to vilify whites and stop the "stand your ground" laws. It is, in fact, an effort to stop ALEC, an organization that has opposed the welfare state and ethno-centric favoritism for many years. It is not a racist organization. In addition, the effort to ensure that honest citizens can protect themselves without civil liability is not part of a racist intent to kill "innocent" black people. It is an effort to ensure that people, any people, of any color, can protect themselves in cases where they are being attacked - without having to worry that later they might be accused of criminal murder for defending themselves or sued civilly for having harmed or killed their assailant. "Stand your ground" laws protect innocent people against predatory lawyers seeking to squeeze money out of them for crimes committed against them.

Jones's assertion that "stand your ground" laws are racist, if heeded, will have the effect of releasing criminals onto the streets to "kill at will". Without "stand your ground" in effect, a criminal can expect that anyone he attacks will have no legal standing for defending him or herself in court. In effect, "stand your ground" protects innocent people from assault because the criminal will know that such a citizen can protect himself and that the law defends his right to do so. If the progressives were really concerned about violence on the streets of, let's say, south Chicago, they would be overwhelmingly in favor of "stand your ground" laws.

We must understand what Van Jones was doing. He was trying to destroy civility and reasoned debate in society in order to replace it with mob rule, mob lynching and other forms of violence. The outrage expressed by many race baiters in the Trayvon Martin case was being stoked and aggravated in order to create disorder and violence on the streets. This was not about Trayvon Martin or George Zimmerman. This was about a deliberate effort by the radical left to breakdown improving race relations and destroy civility for the sake of power. This effort would grow in the wake of events in Ferguson, Missouri and Baltimore, MD where the Black Lives Matter crowd tried to encourage additional violence and the murder of police officers.

I was asked what I thought was going to happen if people start believing that all white people are racist. I answered: "There is only one thing that could happen when collectivism becomes the common method of thinking: lots of dead bodies. That's what happened in Germany when Hitler started railing against the Jews. It was the illogical and unscientific "group-think" that gave Hitler the justification for jailing and murdering Jews. And this is the same method that Jones and his radical friends in BLM are trying to smuggle into our society. What's the next line? 'Whites are racists; we must get rid of them'." And, in fact, many of the radicals have been saying exactly that for several decades. All they need is a good lynch mob atmosphere to get it done.

The worst aspect of this travesty is that Republicans are clueless about the race warfare that people like Jones are trying to bring about. The only people who seem to understand it are the black conservatives who have spoken out; Thomas Sowell[19], Shelby Steele[20] and a few others. They are warning us about these radicals and their destructive goals.

When you consider that George Zimmerman, the man accused of murdering Trayvon Martin, is a Latino, not a white person, that all the media "evidence" that was used against him (the evidence that started the so-called outrage), was selectively edited, you have to ask yourself about the immoral nature of people who would take advantage of a situation like this in order to create a lynch mob mentality, not just on George Zimmerman, but on every non-black American in the country. This is utter evil, and because of it, we are moving into a dangerous time for the nation. The real racists are those who are stoking the fires of this issue and they must be called to task.

Radicals like Van Jones are not engaged in a war to help blacks or even to protect them. Their war is against the individual, the one person who must be enslaved in order to advance the entitlement state. This person must live in

---

[19]http://www.nationalreview.com/articles/294456/geraldo-and-hoodies-thomas-sowell
[20]http://online.wsj.com/article/SB100014240527023033025045773236911349263000.html

fear about whether tomorrow he will be robbed on the street or robbed by his government.

Collectivism is the means of creating fear in individuals and of forcing them to give up on a better life. One thing is sure, in this environment today; if you are white, don't count on being in the right group. It doesn't matter that you are a fair minded, hardworking individual who has treated all people equally. The only thing that matters is that other whites were racist and, well, you're white. This is the essence of collectivism.

Racial division is the goal of Van Jones and our present government: If they can spread the poison of collective thinking, as did Hitler; if they can get you to think in terms of groups, then they can justify anything. If you really want a civilized society that gives everyone a fair chance, you cannot allow them to use race to divide us. The idea that groups matter over individuals is the lie that Hitler and the Nazis brought to the world. The result was a devastated world and millions of murdered individuals. On the basis of racial group thinking, the logical fallacy known as overgeneralization, fascists can direct the debate to favor any group they choose and disfavor any group they'd just as soon do without. This process enabled Hitler to gain the trust and loyalty of Germans and the deaths of other people who were not part of that group. Is Van Jones the next Adolph Hitler? Only you can make sure that he is not.

Speak out and let people know that this nation is about individuals not groups, that it should focus on individual rights not "social justice". This is a society based on laws, not on men who hold the power of life and death over other people.

The President's Gimmick

"What was true then can be true now. Our unique strengths as a nation — our optimism and work ethic, our spirit of discovery and innovation, our diversity and commitment to the rule of law — these things give us everything we need to ensure prosperity and security for generations to come.

"In fact, it's that spirit that made the progress of these past seven years possible. It's how we recovered from the worst economic crisis in generations. It's how we reformed our health care system, and reinvented our energy sector; how we delivered more care and benefits to our troops and veterans, and how we secured the freedom in every state to marry the person we love.

"But such progress is not inevitable. It is the result of choices we make together. And we face such choices right now. Will we respond to the changes of our time with fear, turning inward as a nation, and turning against each other as a people? Or will we face the future with confidence in who we are, what we stand for, and the incredible things we can do together?"[21]

How can a President who trades in untruth win an election? Does he not know that you can't solve our nation's problems by focusing on non-essential traits such as "optimism"? This approach precludes a discussion about the fundamental traits that make it possible for

---

[21] President Obama's 2016 State of the Union Address

Americans to muster strength against difficult odds. Like the Germans under Hitler, who were told that their essential characteristic was their willingness to sacrifice for the "volk", the American people are feeling the burden of massive deficits, constantly rising prices and an inability to know how to right the nation's course. As they watch their incomes buying less each week, they will have to lower their expectations, reduce spending and eat less. Where will their optimism go then? Will they continue to feel that life is a great adventure and that anything is possible?

In fact, the President's appeal to optimism solved nothing. People cannot be optimistic when they are bleeding to death. When people are called to sacrifice more and more with each government failure, eventually, people give up and the President will declare that they are not good enough for his grand vision of the future. This has happened in virtually every collectivist experiment in history.

Eventually, people will begin to see that the President is merely using the language of sacrifice in order to launder money for the sake of people who are not required to sacrifice; the cronies in some large corporations, the bureaucrats who determine life and death for taxpayers, veterans and seniors, the leftist organizations that dispense lies and steal elections, the politicians who enjoy yachts and private jets and Caribbean chalets; and even the poor who receive sustenance while the producers work a second and/or third shift. They begin to wonder if there is not some gimmick being used on them, some deceptive words that are intended to hurt them in some way.

What will Americans be told when their optimism is gone? As a pragmatist, the President would likely have another gimmick ready. He might take the opportunity to hire his old friends from ACORN, meet with his friends in the unions, his friends at Americorp, his friends at Occupy Wall Street, his friends at Media Matters and put them to work to channel your energy toward, guess what, more sacrifice. By then, he'll have given Americans so many scapegoats who are "responsible" for the nation's suffering that many people will blindly follow his community organizers. By then, many more Americans will be slaves who must march on their orders, protest on their orders, shake down businesses on their orders - for the sake of $40.00 a week of worthless money in their paychecks.

For the President, sacrifice was a magic formula, a benign concept viewed positively by millions. When companies like Solyndra squandered the money your sacrifice had given them, the answer was not to stop giving money. Solyndra's failure is proof that the American people did not give enough money. When the unions destroyed large industries through high wage demands, Americans are told the cause of bankruptcy was not enough bailout money for GM. More sacrifice always fixes too little sacrifice according to the President. And the spiral goes down, down, down, across a whole country that blindly demands more of what caused the problem.

The President does not seem to realize that sacrifice is a failed idea. Even now, in 2016, he has yet to question the discredited ideas of Kant, Hegel, Marx and Engels, each of whom preached duty and sacrifice. Like Francis of Assisi, the monk who seldom bathed, he thinks sacrifice brings great benefits and solidarity to mankind. He ignores the decay of the Dark Ages ruled by Christian sacrifice. He's forgotten the killing fields of the most altruistic societies in history such as Nazi Germany and Soviet Russia and Communist China. His friends are far left fascists who reject the Constitution and think that good government is re-distribution. Like many American intellectuals, he refuses to see that the negatives associated with sacrifice are worse than any of the possible benefits. He is swamped by technocrats who think they know better what the people need. Yet, they do not have the intellectual acumen that would bring them to question the idea that men should be forced to sacrifice. For them, the need for sacrifice is a foregone conclusion, an idea so logical, that it should not be questioned. As typical altruists, they do not realize that the essence of altruism is that it demands suffering.

One of the most deceptive aspects of altruism includes many of the President's favorite themes. These themes represent the "escape clauses" of altruism; the methods of deception that give "credibility" to the idea of sacrifice and make it seem to be about helping others. Altruists routinely equate sacrifice with such concepts as love, benevolence, helping those one loves, kindness, generosity, voluntary charity and other concepts that have nothing to do with the idea that men must be forced to give up their lives, energy, money and profits for the sake of those who have not earned them. Altruism claims to be about helping people, but throughout history, it has lambasted honest, hard-working people by calling them selfish and exploitative. Altruists of the past have even jailed, hanged and tortured people for the mere act of trying to survive. This is the essence of altruism: hating people and wanting to see them suffer. It is about ridiculing the successful and stealing their success. It is about the destruction of the human mind, confusing people, making them feel guilty and berating them for self-interest. It is about preaching optimism in the face of the very despair that the President has given them.

The President routinely equates sacrifice with the success of our country. He interprets the work that Americans have done for themselves and their families as sacrifice and claims that this "sacrifice" made America great, not individual initiative, not individual rights, not economic freedom. This attempt to switch the founding principle of our nation from freedom to sacrifice is the gimmick that the President uses when he proposes more sacrifice. He seeks to turn our nation away from individual rights toward a fascist system where the government plays referee, decides winners and losers and buys votes by punishing honesty and ambition.

Certainly a person of the President's knowledge and intellect knows that history has shown altruism to be the means of looting societies. History has shown that the failures of the sacrificial state have only been met by more sacrifice and that the people are eventually left destitute. Is he that mentally addled that he cannot see the consequences of sacrificial societies? Where is the wisdom that has characterized so many men who have sat at his desk? Is his gimmick an intentional act of deception or is he merely disconnected from reality? Perhaps we should question his mental powers, his psychology.

Does the President know that altruism is the means for destroying individual rights? Does he know it destroys the human mind? Does he know it destroys success? Does he know it destroys prosperity? Does he know it requires scapegoats and that it destroys those scapegoats? Does he know it has left killing fields full of millions of skeletons for decade upon decade? Does he know it has never created an affluent society? Does he know it destroys his vaunted American optimism? How could he not know?

But then, shouldn't you, the voter, also know it? As an American who must decide about your nation's future, why haven't enough of you resisted the President's call to sacrifice? Why haven't you realized that the President's gimmick, his call for a morality of sacrifice, is a call for the destruction of America?

The truth is you have always been told that sacrifice for others is good. Like the generations of many past dictatorships, you stand mute when someone proclaims that you haven't worked hard enough for the people. Haven't you been taught that it is your duty to sacrifice for others? Haven't you heard repeatedly that capitalists are greedy, money grubbers, thieves and charlatans? The President is only telling you everything you "know" from your upbringing. Where's your willingness to sacrifice for the noble cause of the President's political base? Why aren't you part of that political base? How can you disagree? What kind of person are you to think that greedy materialistic avarice can possibly be superior to pure, godly, sacrifice for your fellow man? Where is your optimism for the cause of sacrifice? What kind of monster are you to disagree with the President? How could you possibly defend the rich?

Needless to say, I ask these last questions with my tongue in cheek. But it is true, that if an idea is moral, there is no reason to be inconsistent; in fact, it is immoral not to live your moral code. If altruism is moral, what are you doing living for yourself, feeding yourself and caring about those you love? How could you be so selfish? Why don't you jump onto the first sacrificial pyre that you come upon?

Let's not be so quick to give it all up. It is true that once you identify a proper morality, there is no reason to act against it. But we must ask the question; is altruism really a good morality? Is it even possible to be consistently good under such a system? How can a "good" morality require that man die in order to be moral? I submit that altruism is immoral and the President's insistence on building a society based upon sacrifice is also immoral. The dominance of altruism in our society is due to the dominance of both religious and empiricist philosophers such as Hume, Kant, Comte and other secularists who infused their systems with the morality of altruism. Religion created the religious conservatives while the secularists created the progressives. Both groups believe that man should sacrifice, one to God and the poor, the other to the state and the poor.

Most politicians today tie their political positions to altruism and, as pragmatists, they see the proclamation of strong religious belief as essential to political success. President Obama is no exception. In fact, he recently gave a speech where he tried to attach his political advocacy of altruism in government to his Christian faith. Gone are the days when a Presidential candidate would proclaim that his religious beliefs would never touch his respect for the Constitution (Kennedy). Today both Democrats and Conservatives eagerly proclaim that their religious beliefs animate and inform their political decisions. Constitution be damned.

The President said:

"But in my moments of prayer, I'm reminded that faith and values play an enormous role in motivating us to solve some of our most urgent problems, in keeping us going when we suffer setbacks, and opening our minds and our hearts to the needs of others."

Here the President betrays what many people have thought of his economic policies; that they are not based in provable facts and reality, but upon "faith". He relies on ideas that he cannot support by reason and logic. We are now being led by a man with his eyes firmly closed to reality. Why hasn't the President studied how men survive in society? Why hasn't he tried to define the fundamental facts that would cause men to prosper in society? What is his theory of man and how does it relate to the concepts of individual rights? What are rights and how are they derived from reality?

These questions are being ignored by the President because he seems to think that prosperity comes out of a vacuum; that men work hard because it is their duty; that men think high thoughts and derive broad abstractions merely by wishing. He seems not to understand the role of reason in society and the importance of objective law. He believes that society is successful only because of the manipulations of moral authorities who steer men toward "social justice" through sacrifice. The President's example of a moral authority appears to be the coercive technocrat such as a Czar.

Yet, the President talks about his values and how important they are to him. He continues:

"We can't leave our values at the door. If we leave our values at the door, we abandon much of the moral glue that has held our nation together for centuries, and allowed us to become somewhat more perfect a union.

Frederick Douglass, Abraham Lincoln, Jane Addams, Martin Luther King, Jr., Dorothy Day, Abraham Heschel -- the majority of great reformers in American history did their work not just because it was sound policy, or they had done good analysis, or understood how to exercise good politics, but because their faith and their values dictated it, and called for bold action -- sometimes in the face of indifference, sometimes in the face of resistance.

"This is no different today for millions of Americans, and it's certainly not for me."

When the President says, "We can't leave our values at the door", he means that he is obliged to impose his values on you regardless of what you think or even whether his values violate your values. It is a dangerous position to hold in a diverse society. Yet, the President's values, he claims, "are the glue that has held our nation together for centuries." This is an effort, because of the President's 'bully pulpit', to define those values for the rest of society and to ensure that there is no opposition to them. What makes his statement even more problematic is the assertion that this "moral glue" is the sole reason that has "allowed us to become somewhat more a perfect union." This "social glue" to which he refers is a very un-American idea called "collectivism".

Yet, the President's statement that these reformers created an "almost" perfect union seems to represent a complaint of sorts. This reminds us of the statement once made by the President in a radio interview in which he declared that the framers of the Constitution somehow failed to provide for re-distribution in the Constitution. Needless to say, this view represents a serious departure from the very intent of the Constitution. The framers did not intend to provide for re-distribution; they omitted such a concept because they held that it was not the proper role of government to re-distribute anything.

Apparently, the President thinks re-distribution is "sound policy". The reformers he mentions did what their faith demanded; and even more importantly, their faith dictated "bold action". The President is telling us that his very own "bold action" is dictated by God and morality. He must advance re-distribution, his "sound policy", because, in essence, God demands it and he is a good Christian.

That this idea violates the essence of limited government seems to be overlooked by this "Constitutional Scholar". In fact, it is prohibited by the Constitution for the President to make any law concerning religion. For him to impose his religious demands for sacrifice violates the Bill of Rights. The Founders specifically prohibited the government from violating the rights of citizens, even if that violation is called for by God.

In fact, the Founders did not consider it to be "sound policy" or "good politics" to buy votes by means of doling out the citizen's money to political friends and allies. The idea of re-distribution is a wedge that introduces division and chaos into society. But the President feels compelled to impose his views regardless of indifference or resistance because God demands it. How "good" of him.

"I wake up each morning and I say a brief prayer, and I spend a little time in scripture and devotion. And from time to time, friends of mine, some of who are here today, friends like Joel Hunter or T.D. Jakes, will come by the Oval Office or they'll call on the phone or they'll send me an email, and we'll pray together, and they'll pray for me and my family, and for our country.

"But I don't stop there. I'd be remiss if I stopped there; if my values were limited to personal moments of prayer or private conversations with pastors or friends. So instead, I must try -- imperfectly, but I must try -- to make sure those values motivate me as one leader of this great nation.

"And so when I talk about our financial institutions playing by the same rules as folks on Main Street, when I talk about making sure insurance companies aren't discriminating against those who are already sick, or making sure that unscrupulous lenders aren't taking advantage of the most vulnerable among us, I do so because I genuinely believe it will make the economy stronger for everybody. But I also do it because I know that far too many neighbors in our country have been hurt and treated unfairly over the last few years, and I believe in God's command to "love thy neighbor as thyself." I know the version of that Golden Rule is found in every major religion and every set of beliefs – from Hinduism to Islam to Judaism to the writings of Plato.

"And when I talk about shared responsibility, it's because I genuinely believe that in a time when many folks are struggling, at a time when we have enormous deficits, it's hard for me to ask seniors on a fixed income, or young people with student loans, or middle-class families who can barely pay the bills to shoulder the burden alone. And I think to myself, if I'm willing to give something up as somebody who's been extraordinarily blessed, and give up some of the tax breaks that I enjoy, I actually think that's going to make economic sense.

"But for me as a Christian, it also coincides with Jesus's teaching that "for unto whom much is given, much shall be required." It mirrors the Islamic belief that those who've been blessed have an obligation to use those blessings to help others, or the Jewish doctrine of moderation and consideration for others."

The President has no problem being the person who decides what will be required. His faith tells him that the burden of ensuring that seniors are taken care of and that families can pay their bills falls on those to whom much is given. But here's where faith is not enough and simple mathematics should take over. There aren't enough productive people to ensure that seniors are given their retirements; that the poor have homes, educations, health care, child care, contraception, unemployment checks. But these facts don't matter; what matters is sacrifice, not because it is practical, but because God demands it. There can never be too much sacrificing.

There is something even more wrong and disconnected in the President's words. In his "reality", "shared responsibility" is not evenly shared. George Soros and General Electric have less responsibility to share than you. Unions now virtually own car companies and private investors have been cut out of their investments in those car companies. The President is not with those investors, he has declared. It seems they must share their responsibility but the unions must not.

The enormous deficits of the last seven years were caused by the President, not George Bush. And the fact that families cannot pay their bills is due to the President's Quantitative easing that is causing monetary inflation and rising prices. The President has brought forward stimulus plans that haven't stimulated and Green Energy investments that have produced little green energy; all with the sacrifice of trillions of dollars.

Merriam-Webster defines schizophrenia as "a psychotic disorder characterized by loss of contact with the environment, by noticeable deterioration in the level of functioning in everyday life, and by disintegration of personality expressed as disorder of feeling, thought (as delusions), perception (as hallucinations)...." I am not a psychiatrist but I think it is a good question to ask whether the President is connected to his environment (reality). For him to base his actions on ideas that have no foundation in reality is a real problem for those of us who must deal with reality. And certainly, not to care about the well-being of those Americans who must pay for the massive deficits through taxes and rising prices (the tax of inflation) must certainly amount to a "disorder of feeling" especially when you consider the numerous golf games, vacations, and some of the lavish parties at the White House.

The President thinks his faith should determine his actions; yet his actions create the opposite of what he envisions – they are creating more poverty not abundance; the world is not made a better place and the President disregards the consequences of his policies and their impact on the lives of real living human beings. If this is not a "disorder of feeling" and a lack of "contact with the environment", I don't know what is. Certainly, many people on the left have talked about "pulling together". It is a high value for them especially if people actually do it. They smile at their own brilliance, oblivious to the fact that the left has been waiting for centuries for these ideas to actually work. They will be waiting tomorrow as well; and tomorrow, and tomorrow and tomorrow.

As a youngster, I lived through the 1950s, I remember one of the strongest arguments against communism. Americans of that age learned that communism was founded on the Marxist injunction "from each according to his ability to each according to his needs". This injunction was viewed by most Americans of the 50s as totally impractical. It was this very idea that made the

Soviet Union into a failed society. Americans knew that this Marxist idea did not work and they typically branded communism as evil and impractical. Today, the President thinks that sacrifice (re-distribution) is a magic formula for abundance and prosperity, that spreading the wealth creates new customers for the economy, completely oblivious to the fact that this very idea caused dictatorships to collapse in virtually every case. If this is not a lack of "contact with the environment", I don't know what is.

Yet, the President is right in one respect; if you believe in altruism, you must impose it politically. You must see its establishment as more important than individual rights. You must understand that altruists should ignore the pleas for freedom by those who are supposed to sacrifice. Given the definition of morality fostered by both the President and the Republicans, the President is being more consistent. After all, sacrifice for others is considered to be "moral" and the moral is the good. It is an "either/or" issue. The Republicans have always wanted a government based on Judeo/Christian principles and this is what the President has given them. Were they consistent with their own altruistic beliefs, they would agree with the President and attempt to bring society in line with the "good".

This is why Republicans lose elections. They are not a true opposition movement. They hold the same basic false premise (altruism) as the Democrats. Either the Republicans are going to have to take the opposite position and foster individual rights or they should join the Democratic Party.

The real dilemma for Republicans is that their middling advocacy of altruism does not represent the philosophy upon which this nation was founded. People like Glenn Beck and others play into the hands of the progressives when they agree that "sacrifice" is our fundamental philosophy. The President, when he says that sacrifice is our core value, knows that the Republicans cannot disagree with him.

Over the next few months you'll be bombarded by the call to sacrifice and you'll be told over and over that altruism/sacrifice is a core American value. You'll be asked to sever your contact with reality and to sanction the President's policies that he prays about every day. You'll feel so guilty for trying to survive that you'll wonder how you ever got into a position in life where you are in favor of greed, theft, racism, torture, inhumanity and downright murderous evil. How could you vote against a man who is trying to do so much good, who is trying to help so many people? How could you vote for a Republican who is the epitome of avarice and greed, the defender of capitalism, the crony of fat cats and who'd rather give a tax cut to a rich person than a government program to a baby starving in the cold streets? What kind of person are you?

Oh, you're a Republican.

You'll have to agree that the President honors real American values when he tells you:

"Well, I'm here to say they (the Republicans) are wrong. I'm here to reaffirm my deep conviction that we are greater together than we are on our own. I believe that this country succeeds when everyone gets a fair shot, when everyone does their fair share, and when everyone plays by the same rules. Those aren't Democratic or Republican values; 1% values or 99% values. They're American values, and we have to reclaim them." (parenthesis mine)

The President here is reminding you that good ethics is sacrificial ethics. He will repeat those words above incessantly about "a fair shot", "a fair share", and playing by "the same rules" so many times because focus groups have told his pollsters that they work, they ring true.

Who would be against getting a fair shot? What is a fair shot? In the President's mind a fair shot is a chance to be given the money necessary for a college education, food stamps, unemployment assistance, rent assistance, contraception, child care assistance and health care. All of these things can help the poor stand equally in the competitive race to succeed in society. They will be provided by those who are not giving their "fair share".

Paying a fair share means that more will be demanded of those who have higher productive ability. Playing by the same rules means those people with productive capacity should be regulated by government so they don't exploit those people without productive capacity. In many cases, this means that some products, (such as oil) will not be available. If you notice the contradiction between a fair share and playing by the same rules, it is not the President's fault that you're a selfish monster.

Of course, I don't think you're a selfish monster. But we must ask the question: is sacrifice for the collective really an American value? No. It is an evil idea that destroys values and forces men into slavery.

The President has no problem with you working hard, being self-sufficient, even a genius, as long as you, the producer, are subjected to social justice. If you accept the lie that you really didn't accomplish your success on your own; that you were made successful by those who are not successful, that others sacrificed to give you roads to carry your products over, then you understand what it means to be part of a "social contract". Work hard, yes, but give some to others. Get a fair shot, but don't take more than those who haven't had a fair shot. Play by the same rules but don't take advantage of your higher success; make sure that others don't suffer from your success; give part of your product to others. This is the anti-self-sufficiency philosophy known as social justice. This is from each according to his ability to each according to his need. Oh, did I say that? Did I just remind you how communistic that idea is? This is the "fairness" of President Obama and, for many decades, Republicans have always said, "me too."

The Tea Party movement came into existence because of the President's policies. The Tea Party protesters saw that individuals in the middle class were not getting a fair shot. They realized that while their work was providing the goods, their money was being stolen by means of the Community Reinvestment Act, high oil prices, TARP, massive "stimulus" packages that stimulated nothing, massive deficits and inflation. Their IRAs and 401Ks were being raided, their money was being devalued. Where was their fair share? And where are their same rules? And, how can a nation possibly succeed when it vilifies the "good" people who make money and pours that money down the throats of the non-productive? The President thinks these people should "work together" under his leadership while their money goes down the drain for the sake of Solyndra, Goldman Sachs, General Electric, the unions and sundry other looters who think they are too big to fail and that you are too small to complain.

How could you complain? How could you side with the evil rich who made it without government? How could you be in favor of starvation?

The truth is that altruism is based on a false and evil moral philosophy. Social justice is reverse-justice, just as every statement made by progressives is a reverse truth, a lie. It is a violation of the principle of equality before the law, not only because it violates individual rights, not only because it represents slavery, but because it treats some people differently, it loots and exploits people with ambition and a desire to succeed. All those people that the President feels sorry for; they are suffering because of his policies.

Altruism destroys the principle that a person has a right to the pursuit of happiness. The President is wrong when he declares that altruism is foundational in society, when he declares that "togetherness" is how we became a great nation. Altruism institutionalizes collectivism, the premise that groups are paramount in society and that one group, the poor, has a claim on the production of another group, the so-called rich. This principle is false, evil and un-civilized; it is the essence of plunder and theft. It is the destroyer of optimism.

I've mentioned before that altruism is a destructive bomb bigger than the atomic bomb. We are having that bomb dropped on our heads every day with every act and every utterance of the President. Over the next few months, you'll have enough of it. And you'll have to ask yourself if the President is playing some cruel trick on you, trying to disarm you against the theft of your property and rights.

Will you realize that you are a sacrificial victim? Will you join those who have been corralled into concentration camps, incinerators and mass graves by past statist regimes? Or will you be the first generation of revolutionaries who realizes that sacrifice does not build great societies but instead makes dead societies? Will you realize that the message to be broadcast thousands of times with billions of dollars in advertising, has been massaged, perfected and refined, but is nothing more than the ancient call to die for the sake of others, to put yourself upon the altar and to let them tear out your heart for the sake of the collective? Will you realize that self-sacrifice leads to your death? Will you realize that self-sacrifice promises a glorified future that has never come about? How much have you lost because of your sacrifice?

Our Founders realized some very important principles. First, they realized that monarchy was dictatorship/tyranny. They realized that men are never happy in such a system because they are constantly being put upon by government to sacrifice their work for the glory of the king or government. They realized that these forms of government had always wreaked havoc on people, had killed them, ruled them, stolen from them and educated them to be servile slaves. They realized that the only principle that liberated people was the idea that the individual had a right to his happiness; he had a right to keep what he produced and had a right to deal with men without the imposition of force by government. It was a revolutionary idea. But it made possible happiness for any citizen who was willing to work for his own survival. Keeping your money meant you could enjoy your life, have leisure and relaxation...without guilt and without the need to feed the world.

Today, the President wants you to forget that "the pursuit of happiness" means that you can keep what is yours and live without guilt. He also wants you to forget that working without payment is slavery, the evilest idea in history. Why does he want you to forget? Like King George before him, he wants to loot your production for the sake of his friends and he wants you to be the fool who allows it out of a phony moral sentiment.

Are you so weak and servile that you don't see what is happening in front of your eyes? Do you not see the corruption, the lies, the cynical use of altruism to manipulate you? Do you not see that there is no compromise possible with a man who uses lies against you? Do you not see that the charges of "selfishness" and greed are nothing more than rhetoric designed to impose guilt upon you so that the President and his friends can take your last dime?

The President's hope is that you have no ammunition against the call to sacrifice. He hopes that if he talks in glowing phrases about the "value" of helping others, that you'll forget that you have a right to enjoy life. The President is using all the ideas you've been taught against you; and he hopes that you don't have the courage and the moral certainty to say just one word. He'll keep pushing altruism. He'll use all the money given to him by George Soros, the unions, the crony socialists and the sundry rich people who favor communism and fascism and he'll spend it on giving you the message of altruism.

What is that word that he hopes you won't say? It is the word "Why?" Why should you owe your work to others? Why should you work while others do not? Why should your sacrifice mean that you suffer while others benefit?

Why should your money be spent without your approval? Why should you pursue happiness and learn that no happiness is possible? Why don't you have a right to your property? Why is it good to receive from others but greedy to receive from yourself?

Executive Power

"Power tends to corrupt, and absolute power corrupts absolutely." – Lord Acton

Recently, the President made the following statement: "I'm here to say that we can't wait for an increasingly dysfunctional Congress to do its job. Where they won't act, I will."

This statement was intended to reflect the image of an increasingly gridlocked Congress so ineffectual that only an American President could overcome their inaction. Was it true? Was Congress dysfunctional or was the President seeking to denigrate reasoned opposition to his policies? And, more importantly, was the President's goal really to get something done or to turn our nation into a dictatorship?

Was it true then that the President was the only person today with the moral power to act? Was it really as simple as that? Will the history books tell future students about the *courage* of our President or his *deviousness*? Will they examine his deep personal struggle on behalf of the poor or his cynical power play?

We must remind voters that in times past, in particular, during the days leading up to World War II, the European nations had a similar debate. Parliamentary bodies in several European countries were vilified by radicals who favored sweeping aside parliamentary government in favor of dictatorship. During those times, the idea of dictatorship did not have the negative connotation that it does today; it was viewed as a viable option for some nations. Some argued that one man, with the power and charisma to move people, could better implement the will of the people. This man, freed from the shackles of parliamentary weakness, could be the key to making things happen.

Needless to say, two of these men, Mussolini and Hitler, wreaked havoc on Europe, joining a small group of the most hated and murderous men in world history. The absolute power they were given corrupted the entire planet absolutely. Today, we see one-man-rule, not as a saving idea but as a deadly one. At least we did until we got our own charismatic leader with a will of his own. So let's look a little closer at the issue of whether we are becoming a dictatorship.

First, let's examine some important principles upon which our government was founded. The first principle is called "checks and balances". Merriam-Webster.com defines checks and balances as "a system that allows each branch of a government to amend or veto acts of another branch so as to prevent any one branch from exerting too much power."[22]

Notice that the goal of checks and balances is to limit power. No branch of government should have the power to dictate government action, which means to unilaterally

---

[22] http://www.merriam-webster.com/dictionary/checks%20and%20balances

write laws without approval and input from the other branches and from the source of government, the people. In short, unilateral action by any branch or individual is prohibited by the framers of the Constitution. If the President cannot get Congress to act as he would like, then he must desist until he can convince the people of the wisdom of his recommendations. The people would then tell their representatives in the House what laws they should pass. He cannot simply go ahead and act. To do so would violate the purpose of government which is to protect the rights of citizens. Ours is a system of laws, not of men.

You might say that the present situation is too dire to allow Congress to dawdle while people suffer. You must ask yourself, if the President knows this, why doesn't the Congress also know it? Why don't they see the wisdom of the President's position and make an effort to act; to do their job? The truth is that Congress usually also realizes that the situation might be dire and then pass proposals that could be blocked by the Senate.

What the President calls dysfunction is nothing more than checks and balances. The Congress does not agree with the President's "solutions" to the crisis and is therefore blocking his proposals. By doing little about the President's proposals, the Congress is checking the power of the President to act in a way they do not approve. In fact, the Senate in blocking the actions of the House of Representatives is a way for both houses to block the proposals of the President. This is because the people are telling them they don't approve of the President's desires. Doing nothing is sometimes a legitimate response in a free country. This means the checks and balances are working.

Consider that many of the President's proposals had a strong re-distribution component that many in Congress see as harmful to our nation. They point to numerous examples of re-distribution in the past to show that re-distribution causes economic distortions and lost jobs. In fact, a case can be made that re-distribution, as for instance in the subprime crisis, is what caused our economic troubles in the first place. For the President to introduce more re-distribution is analogous to a doctor trying to cure a poisoned patient by giving him more poison.

As Thomas M. Cooley wrote in 1908, "The theory of our political system is that the ultimate sovereignty is in the people, from whom springs all legitimate authority."[23]

This means that legitimate authority does not spring from the President alone but from the governmental body closest to the people; the Congress. If the legislative bodies refuse to pass something the President wants, it in no way means that they are dysfunctional. They are, in fact, performing their constitutional responsibility.

---

[23] Treatise on the Constitutional Limitations...p. 56

To carry the President's logic forward, he was saying that the *people* were dysfunctional, that they lost control of their representatives and that he alone should act on their behalf. Was this true? Remember, in 2010 the people elected a new Congress and Senate and they brought into government a large number of people who campaigned against President Obama's policies of deficit spending, health care and stimulus programs. If Congress was opposing the President's policies and legislative agendas, then Congress was doing what the voters instructed them to do; which was to obstruct the President in advancing his agenda. It was the President's responsibility to acquiesce to the will of the people, to get the message of the last election and to desist from deficit spending, regulatory programs and his health care program.

"Every government degenerates when trusted to the rulers of the people alone. The people themselves are its only safe depositories."[24]

The second principle is called "separation of powers". This is "the principle or system of vesting in separate branches the executive, legislative, and judicial powers of a government."[25] In our system, the executive branch is responsible for seeing to it that the laws of the land are enforced. The House of Representatives is responsible for writing those laws while the Supreme Court is responsible for interpreting those laws when a question of their

---

[24] Thomas Jefferson 1781
[25] http://dictionary.reference.com/browse/separation+of+powers

constitutionality is raised. The Senate is responsible for providing advice and consent to the Executive.

If one branch of government attempts to operate in an area which is not within its range of powers, legal procedures as well as the Supreme Court should intervene and put a stop to it.

In fact, there is nothing in the Constitution about any form of unilateral Executive Power that overrides the laws passed by Congress. For instance, Section 2 of Article 1 delegates to the Executive the power to issue writs of election to fill vacancies of elected representatives. Section 3 of Article 1 discusses additional Executive powers regarding Senatorial vacancies.

Article 2 Section 1 spells out the nature of Executive Power.

"1: The executive Power shall be vested in a President of the United States of America. He shall hold his Office during the Term of four Years, and, together with the Vice President, chosen for the same Term, be elected, as follows"... It goes on to discuss the procedures for the election of the President and Vice President.

At this point in our examination of the Constitution, we've only been told that there is such a concept as "Executive Power" but the Constitution has not yet defined that power. There is no implication that such power is in any way like the power of any other branch or that there are overlapping powers.

We find out what real Executive Power is in the next paragraph Article 2 Section 2:

"Section 2

1: The President shall be Commander in Chief of the Army and Navy of the United States, and of the Militia of the several States, when called into the actual Service of the United States; he may require the Opinion, in writing, of the principal Officer in each of the executive Departments, upon any Subject relating to the Duties of their respective Offices, and he shall have Power to grant Reprieves and Pardons for Offences against the United States, except in Cases of Impeachment.

2: He shall have Power, by and with the Advice and Consent of the Senate, to make Treaties, provided two thirds of the Senators present concur; and he shall nominate, and by and with the Advice and Consent of the Senate, shall appoint Ambassadors, other public Ministers and Consuls, Judges of the supreme Court, and all other Officers of the United States, whose Appointments are not herein otherwise provided for, and which shall be established by Law: but the Congress may by Law vest the Appointment of such inferior Officers, as they think proper, in the President alone, in the Courts of Law, or in the Heads of Departments.

3: The President shall have Power to fill up all Vacancies that may happen during the Recess of the Senate, by granting Commissions which shall expire at the End of their next Session.

Section 3

He shall from time to time give to the Congress Information of the State of the Union, and recommend to their Consideration such Measures as he shall judge necessary and expedient; he may, on extraordinary Occasions, convene both Houses, or either of them, and in Case of Disagreement between them, with Respect to the Time of Adjournment, he may adjourn them to such Time as he shall think proper; he shall receive Ambassadors and other public Ministers; he shall take Care that the Laws be faithfully executed, and shall Commission all the Officers of the United States.

Section 4

The President, Vice President and all civil Officers of the United States, shall be removed from Office on Impeachment for, and Conviction of, Treason, Bribery, or other high Crimes and Misdemeanors."

There is nothing here that gives the President the power to make law, to issue decrees or otherwise make decisions that overlap with decisions that are the Constitutional province of any other branch. It says, simply, that the President "shall take Care that the Laws be faithfully executed". We still do not have any justification for unilateral Presidential action.

It has been argued that the mere mention that the President has "Executive Power" is a justification for unilateral action. There is no reason to make that assumption and any effort to act upon that assumption should be roundly challenged.

A major "power" or responsibility of the President is discussed in Section 7:

"2: Every Bill which shall have passed the House of Representatives and the Senate, shall, before it become a Law, be presented to the President of the United States; If he approve he shall sign it, but if not he shall return it, with his Objections to that House in which it shall have originated, who shall enter the Objections at large on their Journal, and proceed to reconsider it. If after such Reconsideration two thirds of that House shall agree to pass the Bill, it shall be sent, together with the Objections, to the other House, by which it shall likewise be reconsidered, and if approved by two thirds of that House, it shall become a Law. But in all such Cases the Votes of both Houses shall be determined by yeas and Nays, and the Names of the Persons voting for and against the Bill shall be entered on the Journal of each House respectively. If any Bill shall not be returned by the President within ten Days (Sundays excepted) after it shall have been presented to him, the Same shall be a Law, in like Manner as if he had signed it, unless the Congress by their Adjournment prevent its Return, in which Case it shall not be a Law."

Again, we have no justification for unilateral action by the President. There is no mention of an "Executive Order" in the Constitution. Yet, we read elsewhere:

"The president:
• is the Commander in Chief of the armed forces. He or she has the power to call into service the state units of the National Guard, and in times of emergency may be given the power by Congress to manage national security or the economy.
• has the power to make treaties with Senate approval. He or she can also receive ambassadors and work with leaders of other nations.
• is responsible for nominating the heads of governmental departments, which the Senate must then approve. In addition, the president nominates judges to federal courts and justices to the United States Supreme Court.
• **can issue executive orders, which have the force of law but do not have to be approved by congress**.
• can issue pardons for federal offenses.
• can convene Congress for special sessions.
• can veto legislation approved by Congress. However, the veto is limited. It is not a line-item veto, meaning that he or she cannot veto only specific parts of legislation, and it can be overridden by a two-thirds vote by Congress.

• delivers a State of the Union address annually to a joint session of Congress."[26]

What happened? Where did this come from? The only mention of "executive orders" I find in the Constitution is the power to issue pardons and reprieves. Our friends at Cornell try to explain:

"In times of emergency, the president can override congress and issue executive orders with almost limitless power. Abraham Lincoln used an executive order in order to fight the Civil War, Woodrow Wilson issued one in order to arm the United States just before it entered World War I, and Franklin Roosevelt approved Japanese internment camps during World War II with an executive order. Many other executive orders are on file and could be enacted at any time."[27]

So, it appears that "Executive Orders" are justified by precedent alone. Lincoln just began issuing them and no one challenged him (except the south, of course). The fact that Lincoln, Wilson and Roosevelt issued Executive Orders is given as a justification for the acts of any President who thinks it is appropriate to issue an Executive Order. Yet, these Executive Orders, according to Cornell, are issued only during times of emergencies.

We must dissent. Who is to decide that an emergency exists? Why it would have to be Congress, right? If the

---

[26] http://www.law.cornell.edu/wex/executive_power
[27] Ibid

Congress is going to cede power to the President, should it not decide whether an emergency exists? If the President decides when we are in an emergency, what is his constitutional authority for doing so? I don't think there is one. It appears that the framers of the Constitution wanted the legislative authority to reside with the people; so they determined that the power to make law was vested in the House of Representatives. It was not given to the Executive for a good reason; they knew that eventually the Executive would turn that power into a dictatorship. Thomas Jefferson said it best:

"Unless the mass retains sufficient control over those entrusted with the powers of their government, these will be perverted to their own oppression, and to the perpetuation of wealth and power in the individuals and their families selected for the trust." 1812

As Martin and Caul explain:

"The greatest fear the founders of this nation had was the establishment of a strong central government and a strong political leader at the center of that government. They no longer wanted kings, potentates or czars, they wanted a loose association of States in which the power emanated from the States and not from the central government.

"John Adams advocated that a good government consists of three balancing powers, the legislative, executive and the judicial, that would produce an equilibrium of interests and thereby promote the happiness of the whole community. It was Adams' theory that the only effectual method to secure the rights of the people and promote their welfare was to create an opposition of interests between the members of two distinct bodies (legislative and executive) in the exercise of the powers of government, and balanced by those of a third (judicial)."[28]

To understand why "Executive Orders" were not countenanced by the Constitution, we must understand that the Constitution, apart from being a "legal" document is also a moral document. It holds implicitly that the moral is the practical; that free people have the power to make their own decisions and act on their own behalf.[29] It held that individual rights were not only moral but also practical. They were inviolable. Living independently of government control meant living morally and therefore, no single man, not even the President, could hold the authority to unilaterally dictate to any other man. Dictatorship was viewed as an immoral form of government that had disastrous consequences for society.

The Founders saw that individual rights, political freedom and the other rights they acknowledged in the Constitution were issues of morality, issues that reflected the individual's responsibility to himself. So, in order to protect the rights of men to live freely, without coercion,

---

[28] "The Executive Order" http://dmc.members.sonic.net/sentinel/gvcon5.html
[29] For an excellent discussion of the idea that the moral is the practical, read "Capitalist Solutions" by Andrew Bernstein

the branches of government had to be restricted and controlled, powers had to be separated and balanced...as a matter of having a government that respected the freedom of individuals to make their own moral decisions. Coercion, the forcing of a man against his will, was considered immoral and improper, not only when done by one individual to another but also when done by government toward citizens. The idea of one man, not accountable to the people, with the power to issue unilateral orders, to make laws, was considered coercive and dictatorial. Such unilateral action was outside the bounds of proper government. Further, the final check against government power is the power of the people to approve or reject the proposals of the government. Executive Orders eliminate that important check and corrupt the broad principles of the Constitution.

Yet, it was Andrew Jackson who began usurping the Constitution, not Lincoln.

"President Andrew Jackson used executive powers to force the law-abiding Cherokee Nation off their ancestral lands. The Cherokee fought the illegal action in the U.S. Supreme Court and won. But Jackson, using the power of the Presidency, continued to order the removal of the Cherokee Nation and defied the Court's ruling. He stated, "Let the Court try to enforce their ruling." The Cherokee lost their land and commenced a series of journeys that would be called The Trail of Tears.

"President Abraham Lincoln suspended many

fundamental rights guaranteed in the Constitution and the Bill of Rights. He closed down newspapers opposed to his war-time policies and imprisoned what many historians now call political prisoners. He suspended the right of trial and the right to be confronted by accusers. Lincoln's justification for such drastic actions was the preservation of the Union above all things. After the war and Lincoln's death, Constitutional law was restored.

"In 1917, President Woodrow Wilson could not persuade Congress to arm United States vessels plying hostile German waters before the United States entered World War One. When Congress balked, Wilson invoked the policy through a Presidential Executive Order.

"President Franklin Delano Roosevelt issued Executive Order No. 9066 in December 1941. His order forced 100,000 Japanese residents in the United States to be rounded up and placed in concentration camps. The property of the Japanese was confiscated.

"Both Lincoln's and Roosevelt's actions were taken during wartime, when the very life of the United States was threatened. Wilson's action was taken on the eve of the United States entering World War One. Whether history judges these actions as just, proper or legal, the decision must be left to time. The dire life struggle associated with these actions provided plausible argumentation favoring their implementation during a time when hysteria ruled an age."[30]

An argument can be made that none of these acts were proper; that they represented a usurpation of the powers delegated to the President and they violated the intent of the Constitution as well as the oath of office. Certainly, today, most of us see the actions of Jackson as unjustified. He clearly violated the individual rights of the Cherokee people. He used government force against individual Americans which was a criminal act every bit as evil as anything done by Hitler. He should have granted to the Cherokee nation their victory under the Constitution. Through his unilateral decision, Jackson put our nation on a "slippery slope" that is getting more slippery by the day.

But Lincoln had a unique situation. He was involved in the only civil war ever to hit the United States of America. The very survival of the Union, as it was founded, was at stake. One could say that Lincoln needed to protect the integrity of our system and that harsh measures were needed against those who would destroy our nation. Yet, one could also argue that the Civil War would have been won without these Executive Orders. The industrial might of the North and the specific battles won by the North would probably have won the war. Shutting down newspapers may have made little difference to the outcome of the war.

Yet, we must ask ourselves: "If the principles of the

---

[30] Ibid

Constitution are made to apply during peace time, why don't they apply during war?" If the moral is the practical, aren't emergency situations times when we need our principles the most? Were there other legal options that Lincoln could have taken to accomplish the goals behind his Executive Orders? Would these not have been preferable to establishing a precedent that violated the Constitution? Remember, an Executive Order violates the individual rights of every citizen purely on the basis of the fact that it circumvents the power of the people to approve laws. By circumventing this power, the President is circumventing the individual rights of the citizens.

One could also argue that Wilson's order was entirely within his responsibility as Commander in Chief of the military and that an Executive Order was not necessary. One could also say that Roosevelt's order, though a violation of the Individual Rights of Japanese citizens, was also within his mandate to protect the borders of the country (I disagree with that position). Perhaps, not wise, these orders may have been defensible before the Supreme Court due to the responsibility of the President to be Commander in Chief. Perhaps.

What is an emergency that is so important that the Constitution can be disregarded? One has to understand why it is important that government powers cannot overlap; why did the Founders believe the principle was so important that they virtually prohibited the Executive from violating these divisions of powers? And, since they did not identify any circumstance that could be an "emergency" or "exception to the rule", why do we think that such emergencies or exceptions give us the authority to violate the Constitution today?

An Executive Order, if it constitutes anything other than a pardon or reprieve by the Executive, is unconstitutional. The Founders did not intend that the separation of powers and checks and balances should EVER be violated. Furthermore, the violation of these principles was undertaken without justification, without a law enacted by Congress and without the advice and consent of the Senate and, when it was tested by the Cherokee Nation, the Supreme Court agreed that Jackson's Executive Order was unconstitutional.

When a people considers the violation of the separation of powers to be necessary, what is it saying? What is the philosophical implication of such an idea? As mentioned before, the Constitution holds that individual rights are inviolable. It holds that a moral government is one which honors the rights of the people to life, liberty and property. It holds that no emergency could ever justify the violation of individual rights. So how could Jackson, Lincoln, Wilson, Roosevelt and Obama think they could violate individual rights by a mere Executive Order?

The flaw in their reasoning is a long-standing principle that has brought much evil into the world. Those Presidents who issue Executive Orders operate according to a philosophy that holds the moral to be impractical. They hold morality to be self-sacrificial and practical. They see anyone living a "moral" life to be inept and unworthy. In other words, they do not understand that the principles of the Constitution are universal principles that apply to all men for all times and that they create a better, practical and affluent society. They see the moral person as weak. They believe that the principles of the Founders are inferior to a broader, and to them more practical, principle. Their view that the end justifies the means enables them to brush aside the rights and morality of individual men trying to live good lives. They hold, implicitly, that it is proper to violate peoples' rights because only force is practical; only force can accomplish anything worthwhile.

They should ask themselves the question asked by the Founders: Are the coercive acts practiced by potentates, generals, kings, queens and Emperors superior to those of individual freedom and the universal rights of man? Isn't our Constitution telling us that there are no circumstances where individual rights take second place to force exerted by government? Aren't the Founders telling us that there is never a proper time to disrespect men?

We cannot merely say that because Jackson and other Presidents established the precedent of Executive Powers we should not quibble about our present office holder when he continues the precedent. On the contrary, a bad precedent must be overturned and the integrity of the system must be restored lest dictatorship become the order of the day. We must tell our leaders that there is no circumstance that justifies the arbitrary and artificial suspension of our rights. The end does not justify the means.

To understand the danger of Executive Orders and why we must restore the integrity of our system, let's look at some of the Executive Orders that have been issued over the last few years. These examples are provided by Martin and Caul.

"A Presidential Executive Order, whether Constitutional or not, becomes law simply by its publication in the Federal Registry. Congress is by-passed. Here are just a few Executive Orders that would suspend the Constitution and the Bill of Rights. These Executive Orders have been on record for nearly 30 years and could be enacted by the stroke of a Presidential pen:

• EXECUTIVE ORDER 10990 allows the government to take over all modes of transportation and control of highways and seaports.
• EXECUTIVE ORDER 10995 allows the government to seize and control the communication media.
• EXECUTIVE ORDER 10997 allows the government to take over all electrical power, gas, petroleum, fuels and minerals.
• EXECUTIVE ORDER 10998 allows the government to take over all food resources and farms.
• EXECUTIVE ORDER 11000 allows the government to mobilize civilians into work brigades under government supervision.

• EXECUTIVE ORDER 11001 allows the government to take over all health, education and welfare functions.

• EXECUTIVE ORDER 11002 designates the Postmaster General to operate a national registration of all persons.

• EXECUTIVE ORDER 11003 allows the government to take over all airports and aircraft, including commercial aircraft.

• EXECUTIVE ORDER 11004 allows the Housing and Finance Authority to relocate communities, build new housing with public funds, designate areas to be abandoned, and establish new locations for populations.

• EXECUTIVE ORDER 11005 allows the government to take over railroads, inland waterways and public storage facilities.

• EXECUTIVE ORDER 11051 specifies the responsibility of the Office of Emergency Planning and gives authorization to put all Executive Orders into effect in times of increased international tensions and economic or financial crisis.

• EXECUTIVE ORDER 11310 grants authority to the Department of Justice to enforce the plans set out in Executive Orders, to institute industrial support, to establish judicial and legislative liaison, to control all aliens, to operate penal and correctional institutions, and to advise and assist the President."[31]

These orders listed above were issued by previous Presidents. Let's look at some issued by President Obama.

---

[31] Ibid

2009 Executive Orders Disposition Tables
Barack Obama – 2009

Executive Order 13489 Presidential Records
Executive Order 13490 Ethics Commitments by Executive
Branch Personnel
Executive Order 13491 Ensuring Lawful Interrogation
Executive Order 13492 Review and Disposition of
Individuals Detained at the Guantanamo Bay Naval Base
and Close of Detention Facilities
Executive Order 13493 Review of Detention Policy
Options
Executive Order 13494 Economy in Government Contracts
Executive Order 13495 Nondisplacement of Qualified
Workers Under Service Contracts
Executive Order 13496 Notification of Employee Rights
Under Federal Labor Laws
Executive Order 13497 Revocation of Certain Executive
Orders Concerning Regulatory Planning and Review
Executive Order 13498 Amendments to Executive Order
13199 and Establishment of the President's Advisory
Council for Faith-Based and Neighborhood Partnerships
Executive Order 13499 Further Amendments to Executive
Order 12835, Establishment of the National Economic
Council
Executive Order 13500 Further Amendments to Executive
Order 12859, Establishment of the Domestic Policy
Council
Executive Order 13501 Establishing the President's
Economic Recovery Advisory Board

Executive Order 13502 Use of Project Labor Agreements for Federal Construction Projects

Executive Order 13503 Establishment of the White House Office of Urban Affairs

Executive Order 13504 Amending Executive Order 13390

Executive Order 13505 Removing Barriers to Responsible Scientific Research Involving Human Stem Cells

Executive Order 13506 Establishing a White House Council on Women and Girls

Executive Order 13507 Establishment of the White House Office of Health Reform

Executive Order 13508 Chesapeake Bay Protection and Restoration

Executive Order 13509 Establishing a White House Council on Automotive Communities and Workers

Executive Order 13510 Waiver Under the Trade Act of 1974 With Respect to the Republic of Belarus

Executive Order 13511 Continuance of Certain Federal Advisory Committees

Executive Order 13512 Amending Executive Order 13390

Executive Order 13513 Federal Leadership on Reducing Text Messaging While Driving

Executive Order 13514 Federal Leadership in Environmental, Energy, and Economic Performance

Executive Order 13515 Increasing Participation of Asian Americans and Pacific Islanders in Federal Programs

Executive Order 13516 Amending Executive Order 13462

Executive Order 13517 Amendments to Executive Orders 13183 and 13494

Executive Order 13518 Employment of Veterans in the Federal Government

Executive Order 13519 Establishment of the Financial Fraud Enforcement Task Force

Executive Order 13520 Reducing Improper Payments

Executive Order 13521 Establishing the Presidential Commission for the Study of Bioethical Issues

Executive Order 13522 Creating Labor-Management Forums to Improve Delivery of Government Services

Executive Order 13523 Half-Day Closing of Executive Departments and Agencies on Thursday, December 24, 2009

Executive Order 13524 Amending Executive Order 12425 Designating Interpol as a Public International Organization Entitled To Enjoy Certain Privileges, Exemptions, and Immunities

Executive Order 13525 Adjustments of Certain Rates of Pay

Executive Order 13526 Classified National Security Information

Executive Order 13527 Establishing Federal Capability for the Timely Provision of Medical Countermeasures Following a Biological Attack

To be "fair" here's a list of how many Executive Orders were issued by President Bush:

Disposition of Executive orders signed by President George W. Bush:
• Subject Index
• 2009 - E.O. 13484 - E.O. 13488 (5 Executive orders issued)

- 2008 - E.O. 13454 - E.O. 13483 (30 Executive orders issued)
- 2007 - E.O. 13422 - E.O. 13453 (32 Executive orders issued)
- 2006 - E.O. 13395 - E.O. 13421 (27 Executive orders issued)
- 2005 - E.O. 13369 - E.O. 13394 (26 Executive orders issued)
- 2004 - E.O. 13324 - E.O. 13368 (45 Executive orders issued)
- 2003 - E.O. 13283 - E.O. 13323 (41 Executive orders issued)
- 2002 - E.O. 13252 - E.O. 13282 (31 Executive orders issued)
- 2001 - E.O. 13198 - E.O. 13251 (54 Executive orders issued)

291 Total Executive Orders Issued by President Bush.[32]

Do we have an enormous problem here? Were you informed of any of these Executive Orders? Would you have approved them had you been asked? Shouldn't there have been open debate about these orders? Doesn't the issuance of these Executive Orders circumvent the responsibility of Congress to write the laws of the land? Don't they circumvent the responsibility of the Senate to advise and consent? Where is the Supreme Court on this? Doesn't the Tenth Amendment to the Constitution state: "The powers not delegated to the

---

[32] All data found at: http://www.archives.gov/federal-register/executive-orders/

United States by the Constitution, nor prohibited by it to the States, are reserved to the States respectively, or to the people." It does not state that they are reserved to the President.

How is it possible that we have forgotten a key principle of government, the unraveling of which threatens our very freedoms and survival? How can we survive as a free people when the government can do whatever it wants?

Did the Constitution want the Congress to be dysfunctional? The answer is "yes". It did not countenance a Congress that was efficient because it saw "efficient force" as a violation of the rights of the citizens. The framers saw the citizens as the main protectors of their own freedoms and they sought to give the most power to the people as a check on the acquisition of power by the other branches of government.

The framers intended that the government be, in a sense, gridlocked, incapable of doing anything not checked by the people. If the people tell their representatives (through the vote) "no more deficit spending" that meant the Congress could not approve deficit spending. It could not write or pass any laws that enabled such spending. This is the simple practical protection of the Constitution; but the principle that made this possible is the philosophical idea that "all men are created equal", that it was the responsibility of the government to protect, not violate, individual rights. Any violation of the Constitution was a dereliction of responsibility on the part of the violator.

We must understand this issue; so I'll state it again: Any violation of the Constitution is a violation of individual rights. Whenever Executive Orders are issued, the rights of the citizens to approve or reject the actions of government are violated. The Constitution is written to protect individual rights and, one of those rights is the right to check the power of government. An Executive Order constitutes a deliberate dictatorial act against the people.

The proper action for the President, when he decides that a specific government action should be taken, should not be whether to write an Executive Order or ask Congress to write a law. The President's power extends only to the act of convincing the people to act through the legislature. That is the proper challenge put forward by the Constitution. If he cannot convince the people, he cannot issue an Executive Order. This is demanded by his oath of office to defend the Constitution.

Put another way: the Constitution is intended to provide the protocols that guide the proper actions of government. First, the President is required to report on the State of the Union to joint sessions of Congress and he is required to present, during this speech, any proposed legislation he would like to put forward. There is no provision in the Constitution for the President to declare that Congress is dysfunctional and therefore he will act alone. Such a declaration violates the constitutionally mandated protocol for making change; it is a declaration that the people are no longer wise enough to run their government and that their representatives are inept. The statement made by the President that he will act alone was improper. There is no accommodation for such action in the Constitution.

The early Executive Orders of past Presidents added fuel to one of our nation's oldest debates about government powers. We cannot base governmental action on emergencies and I submit that there are other "legal" ways to accomplish proper action without violating the Constitution. Those methods include honoring the intent and procedures established in the Constitution, asking for private action or letting the free market offer solutions in return for profit. If none of these are possible, then leave it the Hell alone.

Government action is supposed to be slow. Most often, deliberation and open debate make for better laws, more thoughtful laws, and they prevent a demagogue from steamrolling his or her own agenda. Having a proper government is important and we must take the time necessary to respond to real problems without creating additional other problems through hasty action. The power of the President to issue Executive Orders outside of constitutional authority must be abolished.

President Obama is the only President in modern times who has openly declared his intent to circumvent Congress. In many respects, especially in his unwillingness to compromise with Congress before and after the 2010 elections, he is involved in an intense war against the Constitution and against freedom. The crisis the President declares is one of his own making; one undertaken, either as a deliberate strategy, or as a haughty response to the outrage expressed by citizens over his deficit spending and Health Care Programs. This made him a dangerous President who should have been confronted in the voting booth and made to desist. The American people should have intervened, or should I say, they should have taken their government back.

To answer the question, "Are we a dictatorship?" the answer is "almost". The President made a serious effort to defeat his "loyal opposition" by discrediting its motives and continuing with his coercive agenda in spite of the will of the people. By declaring Congress dysfunctional, the President was playing politics with our Constitution. If he truly wanted to act for the sake of the nation, he should have desisted from issuing Executive Orders that advanced his unpopular agenda. The people had spoken; he should have listened.

As citizens, we must be vigilant and watch every move made by the Executive Branch. At the present time, the precedent for dictatorship is in place. President Obama took for himself the authority to do anything he desired regardless of Constitutional constraints, division of powers and checks and balances. The only political force that could have stopped him was the people.

The Arab Spring

The next big mistake the President made was to launch the Arab Spring in 2010 and 2011. It was virtually certain, that this movement, whose purpose was to change the governments of several Arab countries, was led by the administration and other groups associated with the Open Society Foundation run by George Soros.

The Arab Spring began with a series of demonstrations whose purpose was to put pressure on Arab governments in the Middle East and Africa to change to a "democratic" model. The President supported these movements because he wanted friendlier, more "open" governments but it is still difficult to understand how he thought that these nations would have been able to established such "open" societies when there was very little intellectual support for them within those countries. Critics, like myself, saw the danger of these countries breaking down into lawlessness while weak puppet governments tried to gain control. The leader of Syria, for instance refused to step down and we have been mired in a civil war there that has cost the lives of thousands of Syrians and left an opening for a virulent terrorist group known as ISIS. The result is that ISIS has captured large amounts of territory in Syria and Iraq as well as other countries.

Libya's revolt sought to displace a dictator who had changed his tune and supported the United States before the Obama administration came along. A policy of "Responsibility to Protect" was launched and even NATO and U.S. fighters got involved. Once the President was captured by militants, he was brutally murdered on video to be seen by the world. Today, Libya is a hotbed for ISIS and sundry violent radical groups held together by a government that has little power. Libya was the subject of an attack in the town of Benghazi that has created a scandal for the Obama administration.

Even Egypt, which had a stable government, became destabilized and the President supported a Muslim Brotherhood member for the position of President and the country seethed with violence for several months until another group deposed the MB government and sent them packing.

Throughout this period, the President tried to rally all Americans to the cause of freedom and secular government in the Middle East. Many Americans saw through this "faux" revolution and knew that it would create chaos in the region. Many wondered how a President who barely had a grasp of what a "democratic" government was could mastermind stable governments in other countries. What was he actually trying to do? Others knew that the entire effort would eventually falter and enable so much weakness in the area that terrorists and new dictators would replace the old more stable dictators. And when the people of Iran decided to engage in their own demonstrations, the Obama administration, for some reason, stood mute.

Many people asked whether the President was supporting true democratic reforms, true American style democracy and freedom of speech, freedom of association...all that good stuff that we can agree about. Many of us saw the contradiction and wondered if his idea of "democracy" was rule by the majority and re-distribution, not republican government. And when the "majority" in Egypt became the Muslim Brotherhood he seemed to care not a whit about American style democracy. What the MB cared about was destroying Israel, brutalizing their women and killing "infidels".

I don't find it strange that the President is using the same language to describe the Egyptian situation that he used to describe his own election. And I'm not surprised that the President mostly ignored American opinion and talked only to the youth of Egypt and America (Occupy Wall Street). And it is not surprising that the rioters also expressed hatred toward American capitalism and the West in general. Wasn't the President the leader of the rioters? Wasn't he an anti-capitalist cheerleader in the states? Didn't he prefer to rule by Executive Order and agency regulation rather than subjecting his policy recommendations to the consent of the people? Isn't he a leader who routinely violated the Constitution and the sanctity of contract which are hallmarks of republican government? Isn't he the leader who apologized to the world for America's "arrogance"? One has to wonder how many other riots in the Middle East and Europe the President and his money man George Soros have lined up for us to watch on Fox News? We later learned that there would also be "grassroots" movements by OWS here in America that proudly asserted that "Capitalism has

Failed".

I also found it interesting that in Russia, Vladimir Putin decided to ban Soros's Open Society Foundation. Apparently, he knows what they are all about; which is destabilizing society under the guise of bringing democracy. I'm sure Putin has seen the contradiction of a group tied to Obama and Soros meddling in the affairs of Russia. Although Putin is a bad character, I am certain he is not stupid enough to let Soros wave around a bunch of hundred dollar bills and hire some willing protestors ala ACORN. Good for Putin. The middle east would certainly be more stable today had they done the same thing to Soros's puppets there.

What do most of the rioters (here and in the Middle East) have in common? It is certainly not religion; it is an abiding desire to destroy capitalism. All of the violent gestures, the loud chants, the anger and vitriol, the threats to cut off peoples' heads off (that means your head and mine) and the beatings are intended to express violent anger at capitalists and what they have supposedly done to the people. All of the playing to the cameras were intended for American capitalist audiences watching from across the Atlantic. They were a threat aimed at America, telling us that they didn't like us for what we have done to the Middle East, which is to provide them with a deep and abiding interest in Egyptian culture and history, Western products, American styles of clothing, computers, cell phones, twitter and Facebook. They have a lot to hate us for.

Yet, I can't help but think that what is going on in the Middle East, even today, is partly a response to the Tea Party protests in the USA that have "transformed" politics and thrown the leftists off their stride. Radical groups who thought that Obama could put them over the top in America were clearly demoralized by the power and capitalist principles of the Tea Party protests. The demonstrations (not riots) of the Tea Party Movement are a direct threat to the left's plans for a takeover of the capitalist system. The Egyptian rioters wanted to send a message to the Tea Party Movement in America that they can change any government at any time through their trained and paid riot organizers. These organizers, once they finished turning Egypt into a Muslim theocracy could hop from country to country until they finish off America...their goal is not only to overthrow capitalism but to gain power...consequences be damned. The Muslim radicals will try to kill off Israel then they will feast on the carcass of America with the President still apologizing for our arrogance and Islamophobia.

I don't find it strange that the administration even told Congress that the Muslim Brotherhood was a secular organization with no ideology, just a bunch of nice guys who want to feed the poor and hungry. Does this mean that the American government supports the Muslim Brotherhood? You have to wonder why they are trying to lull us to sleep about Muslim radicals. At the very least, you can't help but wonder at the involvement of the Open Society Foundation and the remnants of ACORN. They all once felt the sting of the pressure coming from the Tea

Parties. Put it all together and it is clear that the administration is pursuing a policy that will destroy Israel while at the same time setting up the structure that will eventually kill off the capitalists in America - and I mean "kill" in the literal sense. I'm not surprised, are you?

The organizers of the Middle Eastern riots were sending the Tea Parties a message that evil can win in the world if it is organized, morally brutish and violent. Why did they have to go overseas to do this? They can't complain about us here because we'll answer them with reason...so they've gone overseas in order to scare us with the chaos they can create. It is another form of terrorism to try to scare Americans with the implication, "We're coming to get you." They know we're watching. I wonder what the honest people in Egypt think about the manipulation of their country by American and British radicals?

Ameriphobia

During the Obama years, Americans were constantly being told by the left to be more tolerant of people from different cultures; and, especially, not to fear people from Islamic countries. Yet, many Americans have a deep sense of suspicion of some Muslims solely because of the way the 9/11 terrorists infiltrated our country. These monsters insinuated themselves into our lives and took advantage of our tolerance with deadly result. Are terrorists lurking among us still, acting westernized yet working to kill us? Are some of the people who immigrate to America today "sleepers" who will do the same as the 9/11 terrorists? Or are we Islamophobes unduly fearful of outsiders? The President held the latter view.

I don't think our fear of being attacked again is unfounded. It is a genuine fear based upon the fact that many Americans have been killed by religious fanatics in the name of Islam. And I find it curious that we are told by many on the left that there really is no terrorist threat, that the entire issue is stoked up by the right to create paranoia among us and to generate political support for increased military and homeland security spending.

The terrorists were educated by religious leaders, men of God, who breathed venomous hatred toward Americans. Is this still happening? We are told that a lot of this anti-American speech still takes place in many mosques in America. Is our generosity being taken advantage of again? No, we are told, we should realize that our fear of Islamic radicals is a sickness based on our past racist tendencies. Too many of us are Islamophobes they tell us.

I would like to state that part of the problem is the left's insistence on "group" thinking. The leftists are collectivists. They are always talking about "they" and "groups". This is a form of prejudice. As an American, on the other hand, I would prefer to think about individuals, what individuals think and do rather than try to collect people and put them under one label such as "Muslims" or "races". It is individuals who think and act, value and decide. Groups don't think, they don't have collective minds. In fact, even among Muslims there are various types of individuals. Some are secular like most Americans. They go to work every day. Some don't even practice Islam. Some, a very few, are atheists. So it does us no good to categorize all Arabs as "Muslims". You might even be surprised that in the U.S.A. there is a sizable number of Egyptians who are decidedly Christian.

Yet, the question I would ask is "Are we afraid of them or are those Muslim individuals who hate us afraid of us?" What makes so many individuals in the Muslim world want to kill us? Is it their love of humanity or pure unadulterated hatred? Many on the left tell us it is not as simple as that; that there are many factors that contribute to Muslim hatred of America. There is the exploitation by America (unproven) and there is joblessness, lack of inclusion, etc. According to this view, their hatred of us is our fault. I think the President's view would fall under this category.

In pursuit of answers to these questions, I recently read a booklet published jointly by the Council on Islamic Relations (CAIR) and The University of Berkeley Center for Race and Gender entitled "'Same Hate, New Target' Islamophobia in the United States, January 2009, December 2010". This booklet provided an interesting perspective on the question of Islamophobia. In fact, it was more than merely interesting; it was frightening – not for what it revealed about Islamophobia but for what it revealed about Ameriphobia, the unfounded fear of America.

First of all, the article made no effort to scientifically document the existence of Islamophobia in America. There were several anecdotes about anti-Muslim incidents but much of that can be dismissed as non-representative of the vast majority of Americans. Just as you cannot cite a few instances of racism in America to prove racism among the vast majority, you cannot point to a few examples of anger directed at Muslims to indicate a general fear of Islam. It simply isn't fair. But that doesn't stop the CAIR and Berkeley writers of this booklet.

For instance, CAIR's National Director, Mr. Nihad Awad, in his letter published in the article, calls Islamophobia "close-minded prejudice against or hatred of Islam and Muslims…"

This is a flawed definition of Islamophobia. Prejudice is not a phobia. Prejudice is making judgments about a certain person without having all the facts. A "phobia" is an irrational fear. And I submit that no one can provide a scientific study that definitively proves that Americans are irrationally afraid of Islam or that they are fundamentally racist.

What is the point of this definition if it defines nothing? Fear is usually aimed at a person or object that is a threat to the individual's life. Fear of having ourselves or our fellow Americans killed by terrorists is a real fear. It may never happen but it is the fear that is the problem. People who fear change their behavior, they think negatively and they tend not to trust those individuals they fear. But if you call a rational fear a "phobia", you make a person question his fear while you do nothing to alleviate it. You create moral paralysis; you make it impossible for the rationally fearful person to do anything about his fear; you create a clear road for the terrorist and for political groups who seek to undermine America's values and principles.

Add Islamophobia to the tactics of the left and you get the use of the BIG LIE against political enemies. If you constantly repeat the lie that Americans are irrationally fearful of Muslims, it is thought, they will come to believe it. What happens when the "chickens come home to roost"? Mr. Awad's final paragraph tells you, "I pray that in the future, this report will be seen as one element in the movement to push back against individuals and institutions who promote hatred and fear of Islam as an American value." Push back? In what way? For what purpose? How big is this group that must be pushed back and who will do the pushing back? Government, CAIR, Berkeley, terrorists? Will anyone be sent to prison? Will there be street fights and beatings in the push back?

Who are those individuals and institutions who must be pushed back? The report tells us:

• Pamela Geller and Stop the Islamization of America (SIOA)
• Robert Spencer and Jihad Watch
• Brigitte Gabriel and Act! For America
• Frank Gaffney and the Center for Security Policy (CSP)
• Steven Emerson and the Investigative Project on Terrorism (IPT)
• Newt Gingerich
• The four members of Congress who called for an investigation of Muslim Capitol Hill interns
• Osama bin Laden (he was alive at the time), Al-Qaeda and other violent extremists
• Daniel Pipes

I'm not going to give you the biographies of these people. You can look them up yourself. However, I will state that most of these people are critics of Islam who draw a connection between the premises of Islam and the justifications used by terrorists for killing Americans. In other words, they are critics of Islam involved in the effort to understand why we were attacked on 9/11/2001 and since. In fact, none of these people appear to fear Islam. There is no evident prejudice in the arguments of these people; most have made a thorough study of Islam and its tenets. And, with the exception of bin Ladin, most of these people are politically conservative.

Yet, the writers of this pamphlet say this:

"A critical study of Islam or Muslims is not Islamophobic," former CAIR Research Director Mohamed Nimer wrote in 2007. "Likewise, a disapproving analysis of American history and government is not anti-American...One can disagree with Islam or with what some Muslims do without having to be hateful."

Try disagreeing with Islam in Saudi Arabia (without being hateful) or in Iran or Syria or Pakistan or any nation dominated by Islam. And try disagreeing with Islam in America without being called Islamophobic by CAIR.

Who do they consider to be the good people?

- New York Mayor Michael Bloomberg
- Loonwatch (www.loonwatch.com)
- Congressional Tri-Caucus
- Rep. Keith Ellison (a Muslim) (D-MN)
- Jon Stewart, Aasif Mandvi and The Daily Show
- Keith Olbermann and Countdown with Keith Olbermann
- Stephen Colbert and The Colbert Report
- Media Matters for America
- Interfaith Leaders
- Rachel Maddow and The Rachel Maddow Show

This list speaks for itself; but one thing is obvious. Few of these people have ever criticized Islam and some of them are comedians known for making fun of conservatives.

There is no proof that America is a fundamentally racist nation. In fact, it sets the standard for rationality when it comes to judging people according to their character as individuals. Americans, overall, should not feel guilty for their treatment of any group today. The idea of Islamophobia is a concoction of the left intended to impose guilt upon Americans and convince them that they should treat Muslim immigrants differently than they treat American citizens and other immigrants. Rather than analyzing a real issue, offering real solutions that improve society; CAIR and its allies on the left are instead trying to frame the issue to their own political advantage while disregarding true analysis based upon rational standards. They want to politically defeat someone and the key to identifying that someone is our purpose. Who or what do CAIR and Berkeley leftists fear? I'll let you answer that question.

In fact, a good case can be made for the existence of Ameriphobia in both CAIR and Berkeley. This Ameriphobia is not something new, however. These organizations are grounded in a form of anti-Americanism that has existed since the advent of socialism during the 19th Century. One of the biggest reasons that CAIR and Berkeley are afraid of America is that they accept several myths about our system and those myths are founded, not on reality, but on the views, ideas and fears of the enemies of freedom.

These myths represent a strategy designed to denigrate both capitalism and America in order to set the stage for the lynching of America in front of the world. The fact that the strategy is not new is an indication that the members of CAIR do not want to foster understanding and fair treatment. They prefer to mimic commonly used fallacies against America in order to drive a wedge into American society so they can advance their own anti-American agendas. CAIR is an organization that functions as an individual. It has ideas, positions, prejudices and fears. It has an agenda.

The source of Ameriphobia is predominantly Karl Marx. Marx's critique of capitalism is reputed to spell out certain flaws in capitalism that socialism is designed to correct. Marx's anti-capitalism parallels religious ideas found in a number of prominent religions. It is based upon a general antipathy toward commerce, profit and usury expressed by many religions. In fact, the critique of capitalism in Karl Marx's writings is also similar to and parallels the critiques of America expressed by terrorists and many radical Imams today. Most of them get their anti-Americanism from Marxist critiques of capitalism.

These fallacies can be expressed by the following statements:

1. Capitalism is individualistic rather than collectivist
2. Capitalism is inefficient and socialism is efficient

3. Capitalism is Imperialistic
4. Capitalism is decadent and immoral

All of these positions were fostered by Karl Marx and they were propagated in the Middle East decades ago by none other than the Soviet empire as it sought to split off the populace from the governments they were trying to bring under the communist umbrella.

I will not go into the debates over these critiques of capitalism here but I will state that these four statements are false. They are based upon a fundamental idea that self-interest is evil. They are repeated constantly all over the world and especially in American universities where many Muslims come to be educated. They create a massive prejudice among average people all over the world toward America and American businesspeople. They are expressed in American movies by American actors and they create prejudice against anything American. They justify countless unnecessary and restrictive regulations of capitalism and they justify and animate countless violent anti-capitalist and anti-American groups around the world including OWS. These groups and ideas poison the world against self-interest, justify dictatorships and foment hate and destruction. The false Marxist critique of capitalism has devastated and impoverished the 20th Century and stands poised to destroy our economies today. The existence of this critique implicates the leftists in America today as destroyers of freedom and the killers of men.

If you read the arguments of CAIR, Usama bin Ladin, OWS, anti-capitalist Christians, President Obama, Bernie Sanders, Hillary Clinton, Van Jones and others on the left, you will hear these arguments openly, some advocating violence, others advocating government expansion. The anti-capitalists don't want you to know that their solution to capitalism is worse than capitalism. They talk about what's wrong with capitalism and what they are doing to fix it, but ignore the fact that what's wrong with capitalism is that they are interfering with it.

For instance, in the article from CAIR and Berkeley, you hear no criticism of the violations of individual rights in Iran, about Iran's efforts to destroy Israel and destabilize the Middle East. You hear nothing about Saudi Arabia's efforts to foment jihad around the world and especially in America. You hear nothing about how women and other individuals are being killed and maimed all over the world as an expression of "justice" under Islam. You hear nothing about the racism directed at Jews all over the world but especially in the Middle East. You hear nothing about the riots in the Middle East against Christians or about the treatment of Christians who, in many countries, are not allowed to build churches. You hear nothing about the killings of gays and the beheadings of people who happen to have western values. You hear nothing about the dictatorships in Iran, Saudi Arabia, Syria, Lebanon and in the Palestinian territories that are destroying the lives of millions of their own citizens. You only hear that America is evil because it is based on self-interest; that it was once a racist country and that it must reform itself and accept into citizenship people who are decidedly anti-American. And because of the moral implications of anti-capitalism, you seldom hear a protest from American conservatives.

If there are (and I'm sure there are) any truly rights-respecting people within Arab communities in America, they must surely be people who have rejected the barbarism found in their home nations and who have come to America to live as Americans. These people do not like the religious intolerance they have found in their land of birth and they see America as an opportunity to live truly free lives...free of religious dominance and brutality. They come to America to be Americans not Muslims. They don't come to America to hate America. Nor do they fear America. Yet, these people are treated very badly by some Muslims who hate America and fear its freedoms.

CAIR thinks that paying lip-service to American values and expressing an opposition to terrorism, will help them fool the American public. They think they can justify their Ameriphobia and anti-Americanism by fighting a long-lived false image of a racist America. One thing is true: you can only hope to get away with this kind of deception with the help of American university professors.

The title of the pamphlet "Same Hate, Different Target" implicates America as fundamentally racist. To what "same hate" does the title refer? To the struggle by many whites to win equality for Blacks in America? To the many whites, Asians, Hispanics and blacks who have died for the freedom of oppressed people around the world? To the freedom and economic equality sought by millions of immigrants to America? To the Constitutional protections that have been extended to people of all colors in America? No...the article prefers to focus on the racism in America. That's it...we're a racist nation with a cloud of guilt hanging over us. They call us the oppressors of other nations and we must therefore not be prejudiced and hateful toward Shariah Law in America.

The title of this document is an insult to Americans. It rings like an insider comment intended only for people who have a particular point of view. It is a statement that would only be made by someone whose ideology contains a strong anti-American bias. Who are the racists according to this ideology? Why, they're conservatives and Tea Party protestors.

The important question to ask is "What happens when you call American free thinking by the name of 'racism'?" You get a political package deal that gives you the ability to call a difference of opinion full-blown racism. It gives you the ability to demonize people who have no racist intent. For instance, in America, if you make a valid point about Christianity from a philosophical perspective, you are not always called anti-Christian. Nor are you called Christian-phobic. But if you say that most racists during the Civil War were Christians, and that this proves all Christians are racists, you are doing a disservice to religion and to Christianity - and you will be roundly criticized for such unfairness. However, this is exactly what CAIR and Berkeley are saying about Americans who happen to disagree with progressives.

The cultural clash between Islam and America is not between Christianity and Islam. It is between Islam and freedom. The leaders of CAIR appear to know it. Yet, it is true that Christianity is much more acceptable to the average American than Islam and this is a problem for groups like CAIR who are intent on instituting Shariah Law in America. Their strategy is to convince Americans that Shariah can exist side-by-side with Constitutional Law and that it does not represent a threat. But this is not true, the two cannot coexist. The cultural clash is too severe and CAIR knows that Shariah Law represents an attitude that can never be accepted in a society that defends individual rights. So they want us to forget about individual rights altogether and give Shariah and equal footing.

Shariah Law assumes that good Muslims must submit to God and that God is government. Islam was established through warfare and it insisted that any conquered people convert to Islam or be killed. This perspective that Islam is superior to all other religions and all other governments is a direct threat to any nation that has not accepted Islam as government. And, more importantly, in America, it is a direct challenge to the separation of church and state that is vital to our Republic. This conflict can only be resolved by one form of Law superseding the other.

For decades, in America, religion was not allowed into government in order to avoid the tendency of religion to dominate morality and institute religious ritual as mandated practice. The Constitution sought to liberate man from any influence that would circumvent his natural ability to think for himself and it forbade religion from participating in government...even among religious men in government. In other words, religion in America had to accommodate the liberty of man and not seek to impose itself by means of government force. This changed Christianity and made it peaceful. People could be Christian without having to feel that their freedoms were being undermined.

Islam, throughout history, did not have to learn how to "behave" as did Christianity. Today, Islam has burst upon the scene, without the filtering processes inherent in the Constitution, not as a religion of peace, but as a religion of conquest that considers the secular nature of our society to be decadent, this-worldly and evil. Islam did not have to temper itself to accommodate the Constitution because it gained power by conquest in other parts of the world. Throughout history Islam has practiced "cleansing" rituals by forcing other nations to become Muslim. It considers itself to be the true government of man and does not respect the original intent of the Founding Fathers to prohibit religion from being the government. It sees this idea as ludicrous because to them Islam is society and their God is everything.

The result of this approach is not only a disrespect for the principles of America but a belief that America is evil because it has not accepted Islam. Many Muslims see Americans as infidels who sin against God, not because they do truly evil things, but because they live secular lives. The manner of acting that characterizes Americans, their self-assertiveness, their self-confidence, their outspokenness, their way of dress, grooming, their lack of religious piety, even their way of enjoying life, are all problematic for many Muslims. These characteristics are considered an insult to God. This is a clash of civilizations for which there can be no compromise. For CAIR, Americans must realize the devout spiritual nature of Islam, see it as superior morally and decide to submit to it. For many Muslims, there is no other choice for America.

Is it possible that CAIR is trying to use the progressive movement in America as a cover for insinuating Shariah Law? Is it possible that CAIR is asking Americans to consider Islam, a religion that must certainly be in crisis today (due to its inability to control the radical murderers and gangsters among them), as just another group of good citizens who happen to have their own legal system? Is this why Americans are accused of unfairly fearing Islam?

The most important consequence of accepting a poorly defined term such as Islamophobia is that it keeps people from acknowledging their justified fears. It intellectually blocks the real fear people have about terrorism, anti-Americanism and hateful lies spouted by religious fanatics, Islamic fascists and progressives alike. For instance, why does CAIR say that conservatives are Islamophobic when they question the actual implications of Islam and, at the same time, say that Americans must stay silent and listen to all forms of criticism to avoid being called racist? And further, why are conservatives' questions about Islam considered to be Islamophobic but CAIR's mimicking of progressive criticisms of America considered to be patriotic? The article says,

"Among a certain segment of the population, the Tea-Party and right-wing Republicans, anti-Islam bigotry has become mainstream and lost any taboo. People are unabashed and open in their displays of Islamophobia. In large part, this is in reaction to President Obama's election. Many bigots are upset that we have a black president. But because of the taboo associated with anti-black racism, they are constrained from openly expressing it. So they falsely declare Obama is a Muslim and feel comfortable denigrating him for that," said a Muslim who has held elected office."

This is an unabashed lie, a repetition of lies told about the Tea Party movement by the left. Another charge made by progressives that black Congressmen were spat upon and endured racist comments during the health care debate was also untrue. Yet, if CAIR claims to be inclusive of all American opinions, why does it make the same baseless political criticisms as the left makes against conservatives? And what are we to think of the many intellectuals who have made reasoned, scholarly arguments that refute the practicability of the very same progressive policies that are today being advanced by President Obama...classical liberal intellectuals who lived in the 1930s. Are they also racists? How is it that they resented President Obama's blackness before he was born? What are we to think about the people responsible for this report if they are willing to make spurious and false charges such as these?

Remember the list of enemies that CAIR and Berkeley presented in the document? Remember that this list included people and groups that CAIR considered to be Islamophobic. Ask yourself why that list included some conservatives but not the Tea Party movement whose "anti-Islam bigotry has become mainstream". Does this not qualify the movement for that list of Islamophobes? Is it possible that the list was a decoy designed to hide the real enemies who are mainstream Americans?

By now the left knows that it is not going to be able to turn the US government into a coercive state without serious opposition. They realize that the Tea Party movement and many conservatives are, to a large extent, a reasoned, principled opposition that will not allow the destruction of the Constitution. They know that there are too many people who understand the reasons and thinking that went into founding our country, too many who understand the meaning of individual rights, and who will not be silenced or steamrolled by invented "emergencies" and outright lies - or by threats of murder.

Further, organizations like CAIR see the American left as the authors of the cultural diversity ideology that CAIR needs in order to import Shariah Law. They know that they must exploit this ideology in order to succeed; and if Americans reject the concept of cultural diversity, they are in trouble. The Tea Party will not fall for the ploy that a group of people should be allowed to violate the rights of individuals, even those within its group, because of a "divine" law. The Tea Party, for the most part, is decidedly individualistic. They do not consider our nation to be made up of warring collectives vying for control of the government, eager to use government to bash their enemies. Tea Party members judge individuals and encourage individual achievement and freedom. It is a movement of individuals fighting for individuals and because of this, it is an enemy to the numerous collectivists who foster collective solutions, collective sacrifice and collective punishment.

CAIR also knows that American independents, conservatives and Tea Party members will not "go silently into the night". They will not submit to Islam and they will not be cowed by statements of collective guilt. Tea Party members, because they defend individuals, are naturally opposed to Shariah Law and they will not pretend that accommodations can be made between American jurisprudence, group rock peltings and the exploitation, physical mutilation and abuse of women. To Americans, women are individuals and they cannot be summarily abused and controlled.

Our nation is moving into territory that is not new for nations that have descended into dictatorship. Before a dictatorship can take over a country, there must be chaos, violence in the streets and a breakdown of social institutions. This breakdown provides the cover necessary so that the coming dictators can jail, imprison and kill political opposition. To accomplish this, the prospective dictators invent "crimes" that the opposition has committed in order to justify destroying them. Today, we see the hints of the coming dictatorship in the actions of the Obama administration and the things it is doing regarding the Tea Party movement and Republicans in Congress, not to mention the increasing number of unilateral and unconstitutional decisions made by President Obama. The left has found a scapegoat in the Tea Party movement in the same way that the Nazis used the Jews and intellectuals among them, and in the same way that the Soviet communists hated the bourgeoisie and the intellectuals in Russia. In America, the persecuted group will be every single American who is not Muslim.

As a participant in Tea Party protests, as well as an American with Hispanic descent, I find it offensive that CAIR and Berkeley claim to be inclusive, while they criticize without basis a group that is made up of the entire demographic of the American populace. That CAIR aims its accusations of Islamophobia at people whose issues are budgets and excessive government spending should make you wonder at the real issue.

And it is this:

CAIR and Berkeley fear average Americans. They fear us

because we are free to think and judge them. They fear us because we represent a very large swath of mainstream America. They fear us because they cannot credibly call us ignorant anymore; they cannot simply imply that we should be ignored and circumvented. They know we won't allow it. They are playing politics with the very serious issues of our debt, government spending and government waste (the real Tea Party issues) so that they can falsely claim to be a persecuted minority and thereby gain power.

Berkeley leftists know that the political strategy of the left is to marginalize the right by unfairly associating anyone on the right with as many negative concepts as possible including the spurious charge of racism. This is a political strategy that apparently CAIR has no problem with, yet it claims to want fairness and openness toward Muslims and other minorities. We know that no one can fight for the rights of some individuals without fighting for the rights of all individuals. There are no group rights. Apparently, CAIR does not know this.

Most right-leaning intellectuals and even average citizens understand that these tactics are based upon strategies of deception. It is dishonest to demonize your political opponents by means of lies. It accomplishes nothing positive and it deflects honest Americans from the important work of solving our very real problems. The left would prefer to play the politics of destruction rather than solve problems. Why would CAIR want to be part of this deception?

Where is the Islamophobia in the Tea Party argument? In the very fact that it is an argument based upon the principles of our Founding Fathers. In the very fact that the Tea Party movement is anti-progressive. In the implication that Tea Party Americans are so principled that they will not allow Shariah Law to be practiced in America. CAIR knows that with the Tea Party movement around, they can't undermine the Constitution, not now, and maybe never.

The emergence of the Tea Party movement has put a panic into all progressives and CAIR. They didn't expect that anyone would rise up to defend the Constitution. Now they realize that there is a principled movement against them that will not compromise on fundamental principles; and it is a huge movement. They realize that all their arguments for the coercive state no longer work especially the arguments for collectivism and shared sacrifice. They know that eventually they will be swept out of power by this movement in such a large wave that they will be on the outside looking in for the next several generations if not forever. This explains why CAIR and Berkeley kept the Tea Party movement off its list; they didn't want to admit that they feared the Tea Party movement more than any other group. CAIR is Ameriphobic.

CAIR and Berkeley are participating in political games, picking winners and losers, sticking with the progressives and name-calling (Islamophobe and racist) against one of the largest political groups in the country. Instead of calling for objectivity, refusing to take sides in the political struggle, really meaning what they say about fairness, CAIR chooses instead to get into the political fray and attempt to disenfranchise people who care about budgets and Constitutional rights. CAIR and Berkeley are not fighting Islamophobia; they are exposing their own Ameriphobia.

CAIR and the progressives are doomed to fail. This is because past dictatorships have succeeded in gaining power only by tearing down society and cutting off all lines of communication. Today, that would mean they have to destroy mass communication systems such as cable television, the Internet, ebooks, social networking and wireless communications. The freedom that these media rely upon, the freedom of speech, is something Americans are not willing to give up, even if they have no opinion about dictatorship. And, even more importantly, because of its anti-intelluality, the left has been reduced to a few multi-billionaires who waste huge amounts of money funding failed campaigns and bad ideas. The left needs mass communication in order to multiply by several degrees the amount of drivel they need to drown out the truth.

The Tea Party movement is a beacon of hope. In a few short years, the movement has accomplished phenomenal results; they have brought us much closer than ever to restoring the principles of limited government and individual rights. But, unfortunately, it is not an intellectual movement. Although there are strong influences from Ayn Rand and Austrian economics in the movement, it is primarily an alliance of disparate groups that converge on the issues of limited government, spending reductions and capitalism/constitutionalism. These are not bad issues around which to converge but they are not enough to create a free society that endures. In order to establish a proper society, it will take an intellectual movement that effectively defines the philosophical bases of these concepts. That was the work that the Founders, in spite of their superlative accomplishments, left to future generations. It is critical today that our generation do this work.

The Tea Party may succeed in disenfranchising, discouraging and removing from power the radical progressives in government, but before these people can be removed as a cultural force, they must be ousted from the universities. We must win the battle of ideas in order to create a better society.

Changing Change

"Change will not come if we wait for some other person or some other time. We are the ones we've been waiting for. We are the change that we seek."

"Change doesn't come from Washington. Change comes to Washington."

"The change we seek has always required great struggle and great sacrifice. And so this is a battle in our own hearts and minds about what kind of country we want and how hard we're willing to work for it."

"So let me remind you tonight that change will not be easy. Change will take time. There will be setbacks and false starts and sometimes we'll make mistakes."

"We've done this before: Each and every time, a new generation has risen up and done what's needed to be done. Today we are called once more, and it is time for our generation to answer that call. For that is our unyielding faith that in the face of impossible odds, people who love their country can change it."

"I recognize that there is a certain presumptuousness in this, a certain audacity, to this announcement. I know that I haven't spent a lot of time learning the ways of Washington. But I've been there long enough to know that the ways of Washington must change."

"The genius of our Founders is that they designed a system of government that can be changed. And we should take heart, because we've changed this country before."

"When I hear the cynical talk that blacks and whites and Latinos can't join together and work together, I'm reminded of the Latino brothers and sisters I organized with and stood with and fought with side by side for jobs and justice on the streets of Chicago. So don't tell us change can't happen."

"And so if we do not change our politics; if we do not fundamentally change the way Washington works; then the problems we've been talking about for the last generation will be the same ones that haunt us for generations to come."

One thing President Obama never talked about is what he means by the word "change". The question is, what is he changing America into; specifically, what is the "system" he wants for us? Is it a system of constant change such as socialism or fascism? It is certainly not the kind of slow, deliberate change that created the domestic tranquility for which our Founders strove.

Believe it or not, this issue of changing our government was critical to the discussions during our Constitutional Convention in 1787. Our Founders wanted a government that could be changed but only in a very limited, slow, deliberate and thoughtful way; they wanted to secure and strengthen freedom not change it on a whim. They wanted a government based on sound and true principles that corresponded with the real world in which men lived. And, more importantly, they sought to institute "protections" against the government *changing* into a dictatorship. They created the separation of powers, checks and balances, regular elections, property rights, judicial review and even freedom of speech in order to ensure that society did not change into a system where factions such as economic or religious groups could turn the government into a tool of oppression. They wanted a government that secured "domestic tranquility" rather than revolutionary change. They created a republic.

The real issue for the Founders was not how to re-distribute income. They established a government that, for the first time in recorded history, allowed and protected the pursuit of happiness; a system that allowed hard working people to keep the results of their work...by right. They were philosophically grounded in Enlightenment ideas, the development of parliamentary government in England, the experiments of the Ancient Greeks and Roman forms of government; and they carefully pondered how to create something so good and so well constituted that it could not be *changed* easily. Many of their arguments revolved around the question of how to ensure domestic tranquility, peace and cooperation, not division and exploitation.

Something tells me that President Obama would probably have given lip-service to the idea of domestic tranquility. I think he wanted to ensure that people don't correctly understand that the "*change*" he refused to define was really revolutionary change; the kind of change that obliterates and unravels all the work done by the Founders. Revolutionary change destroys domestic tranquility because it is an assault on the Constitution, individual rights and especially property.

Why was President Obama's "change" the opposite of domestic tranquility? First of all, any undefined concept can only do harm. The fact that it was undefined means that those in charge of it can "change" the definition to suit their needs at any time. It is reminiscent of George Soros' "Open Society"; a full democracy where a majority can enslave the productive minority without opposition. In such a "democratic" system, we find that few honest citizens can garner the support necessary to defeat or amend the plundering of their property. A government that has a free hand to disregard individual rights and Constitutional protections can do virtually anything it wants in the name of changing the system to something that it decides is "fair". What you get is what we had with President Obama; a government whose leader ruled virtually by decree without reference to laws or the Constitution.

This "change" society destroys economic activity because business people and private citizens are effectively prohibited from planning their futures. As a matter of survival, they must refuse to invest in the future until domestic tranquility is restored. If they have only plunder of their property to look forward to, they will not produce very much. This is a law of nature, not something you can fix about man. It is a form of justice where honest people refuse to feed parasites.

The truth is that a revolutionary government like Obama's did not see domestic tranquility as a value. Its highest value is *change*. Change is necessary because the leaders do not know what to do and they must have the flexibility necessary to change policies and conditions unilaterally and without debate in order to respond to the unintended consequences of their own policies. Their greatest enemy is the man who expects to be reasoned with and treated honestly. This is why revolutionary governments have always made an enemy of capitalism and capitalists. They have committed virtually every form of crime against these people including murder and imprisonment, disenfranchisement and plunder. Capitalists are the proverbial scapegoats of history, damned by altruism because they pursue happiness and want to live better lives. In other words, they want domestic tranquility and that is something a leader who wants to motivate people toward sacrifice cannot abide. He needs for there to be problems to fix, wrongs to right, changes to make. Change requires agitated people who are worked up and protesting about something.

Revolutionary government needs the ability to steal value through re-distribution, progressive taxation, debt, expropriation, violation of contracts and outright nationalization...in order to get the money it needs to build oligarchs, regulatory agencies, secret police and armies. Revolutionary government requires altruism and self-sacrifice among those it intends to loot and, therefore, it cannot be constrained by such ideas as individual rights and reasoned debate. So the "change" that revolutionary government requires is the destruction of domestic tranquility.

Revolutionary governments, seeking change, necessarily make bad decisions. For instance, our government, under the Obama administration, accepted Keynesian economic fallacies that recommend government re-distribution (through debt) to stimulate demand for products. The false premise of Keynesianism is that government can spur economic activity by giving money to consumers who will then buy from producers. But the money given to the consumers has been taken from the producers, capitalists, factory workers, service employees; and this means that the government is not creating wealth...it is only moving it around (This is why the Stimulus Programs have not created any new jobs). Where producers would invest their money in production, consumers would spend their money on consumption. This creates no new wealth and destroys both jobs and production.

In fact, the government, during the Obama administration destroyed what would otherwise have been rational expenditures of money, diverting those expenditures from the purchase of production capacity to the purchase of snacks, alcoholic beverages and candy. The economy declined because it had been "changed" into a less efficient system. A perfect example of this, if it is implemented, will be the so-called "Cap and Trade" program that will move even more money around and destroy one of the most vital industries we have; our energy industry. This program will tax today's most efficient users of energy and re-distribute money to oligarchs paid by the government to develop inefficient energy products whose prices will be subsidized by the government in order to encourage their consumption. If you thought Fannie Mae and Freddie Mac were failed re-distribution schemes (that brought about a financial collapse) you haven't seen anything yet. This is what you can expect from President Obama's vision of change in America. As of this writing, that policy is being implemented by means of unconstitutional regulatory "rules-making".

The basic fallacy of Keynes and Obama is best expressed by Jean Baptiste Say, "...it is the aim of good government to stimulate production, of bad government to encourage consumption."[33] How does good government stimulate production? It establishes domestic tranquility and leaves people alone to make their own economic decisions. Bad government takes money from the investors and gives it to people who will buy snacks.

Domestic tranquility is promoted when the government is prohibited from violating individual rights, and more

---

[33] Jean Baptiste Say, TRAITE D'ECONOMIE POLITIQUE (Say's Law, that supply creates its own demand was originated in 1803).

importantly, when the government is prohibited from interfering in the private decisions of citizens. When the government can never "change" into a rights-violating government, then the people can freely plan their lives, invest their money, produce abundance and make profits...into the distant future. They require domestic tranquility in order to survive. Our choice is between "change" and decline and domestic tranquility and survival.

It is not likely that President Obama will ever admit that his "change" was the cause of our economic problems. He would prefer to blame capitalism and small businesspeople for being selfish than to admit that his policies have upset our domestic tranquility. He pretends not to see what was in front of his eyes, that his government was doing exactly the opposite of what was necessary for a vibrant economy. His government was "changing" so fast and regulating so much that people did not know how to prepare for the future. He was destroying their rights so fast, spending their money so fast at a level unheard of in the history of the world, that you can credibly ask whether he is deliberately destroying our nation.

The re-establishment of domestic tranquility is not about being a Republican or a Democrat. The Founding Fathers did not think of party divisions or of winning elections when they sought to create the circumstances that enabled citizens to perennially live without the interference of government. Today, we have no such tranquility and the actions of our change-prone government are pushing us further and further into decline. Not only is the private citizen under siege by his own government but the consequences of President Obama's policies will likely make our nation vulnerable to enemies who are intent on destroying us.

We need to restore the time-honored principles that created our society, not because they are traditional but because they are true; they lead to the kind of society where citizens can plan their lives; where they can live secure in the knowledge that they are protected from tyranny. We need to restore domestic tranquility.

In this sense, we need to change change back to the original change.

The President's Achilles Heel

President Obama told us that his Health Care program was unpopular because he hadn't done a good job of communicating the benefits of the program. Then, once again, he recited the same litany of arguments that didn't sway opinions the first time.

He must surely have asked himself some hard questions: why don't the American people want these benefits? What makes people want to repeal the entire bill?

His solution was to put Andy Griffith on the air.

Is it possible that the people are wiser than President Obama on this issue?

The Founding Fathers, particularly Jefferson and Madison, were political philosophers of the highest order. They engaged in far-reaching studies of governments around the world and throughout history. They wanted to create a new form of government that retained all the best attributes of the better systems but which also restricted the negative attributes. They understood the flaws in communism[34], theocracy, monarchy, oligarchy, democracy, to name a few, and they found these systems wanting in their ability to protect men against the development of tyranny. Their solution was a republic that instituted strong restraints on the government such as effective divisions of power, checks and balances, a

---

[34] Via Aristotle's writings on communism, holding all property in common.

written Constitution, a bill of rights and the pursuit of happiness.

The Founders saw any system of government that sought to exploit given groups for the sake of other groups as tyranny. For instance, they did not want the un-propertied mass of people, by vote, to expropriate the property of the rich (re-distribution) and they did not want the rich to use influence with the government to get even more rich (oligarchy). They wanted all groups to be left to their own devices and free of any form of coercion from any direction.[35]

President Obama, on the other hand was not a political philosopher; he was an ideologue who thought that (in essence) a fascist oligarchy with elements of communism (re-distribution) was the best system. He minimized the studied views of Madison and Jefferson and criticized the Constitution because it did not re-distribute wealth. His "system" would bring into government the negative attributes of both democracy and oligarchy – as if it they represented something new that had never been tried. Not only did he hope for the ignorance of the American people about the damage that these systems have caused in the past, he accepted the invalid verdict of Marxist critics that capitalism is exploitation. He considered capitalism to be selfish, wasteful and coercive while at the same time he sought to retain in his own government these same negative attributes.

---

[35] See Federalist Paper #10 by Madison

If he had looked at his own economic program, in particular his Stimulus Program, that produced not a single net job, he should have been asking himself why the jobs were not coming, why he had to tamper with the numbers, why he had to call government hiring for the census an indication of an improving economy. Instead of lying to us, he should have asked why his policies weren't working as he had thought. But he didn't ask that question. Why?

The answer is that President Obama was a committed statist.

A statist adheres to the principle that the government has the moral authority to use force against citizens for any reason whatever. A citizen is considered the property of the state and it is his duty to do as he is told; to sacrifice himself, if the state demands it, for a "higher" good. Further, if the state determines that a particular social goal is a priority, the citizen must dedicate himself to that goal. There is no choice in this matter; the collective rules and the individual's wants, needs or goals are unimportant. If some people have to starve for the sake of the "greater good", that is fine.

Statists consider that leadership consists of passing laws or issuing decrees that the rest of society must obey. They assume that citizens "know" that their decisions are the will of the people. The pragmatic statist thinks that his leadership skill, as a technocrat, is to be found in intelligently manipulating the elements of society in order to accomplish "good" results. He uses college professors who are adept at statistics, and who claim to have a deep knowledge of how society works, to advise him on how to pull the levers of the social machine, to prime the pump, so to speak, and create abundance and happiness all around.

A statist adheres to the principle of collectivism which claims that people, working together, sacrificing for each other, can accomplish great things. They consider that collectivism is the key to winning wars, defeating poverty, eliminating waste and improving the morale of the nation. This too is considered practical. The statist technocrat envisions a world of happy workers, each laboring for the goal of the collective, and contributing to the total product which keeps growing larger. It is all about establishing good morale among the workers.

Which brings us to the next principle of the statist and that is altruism. Altruism is the idea that it is the duty of each individual to participate in the collectivist dream; in fact, that he *must* participate or else he is an enemy of the people. The altruist thinks that if people do not willingly contribute their work, time and lives to the collective vision, they are criminals; they must be punished and ostracized.

The problem for statists like the President is that they are fraught with cognitive blind spots. Their visions blur when it comes to anticipating the final outcome of statism, the point when the gross product is supposed to keep getting larger. The vision of a happy, affluent society, for some reason, never materializes. It must always be pushed off into a further distant future...while the wise leaders figure out how to manipulate the society even more. They look for situations where men are not performing their duties, and they determine how the government can "nudge" them so society can be improved. Each intervention creates more problems and breeds more interventions and takes society to the point where the technocrats lose track of what caused what and how to fix what. The brilliant scholars, now called dunces, are hauled off to prison or summarily purged as enemies of the state. What none of the statists realize is that when you combine altruism with collectivism you end with slave labor, concentration camps and genocide...or revolution.

The most basic blind spot of statists is found in their theory of man's nature. To them, man is an ignorant brute who will always do the wrong thing unless a "benevolent" authority keeps them on the right path. The truth that statist authorities do not see is that man is not a brute, he is a being of volition with the ability to survive by means of his mind. In other words, man has the ability to thrive if he is left alone. This is the fact that the statists refuse to accept and if they *did* accept it, they would realize that statism can never work because it violates the principle that free men create the best societies. This is why every statist society in history has been a dismal failure.

Finally, a statist must also be a mystic who has a reversed sense of cause and effect. Since god thinks and wills miracles into being, the statist assumes without proof that god's way is a better way and therefore god represents the good. For the secular mystic god is society and whatever society decides must therefore also be good and achievable. People should work for it and even die for it. The secular mystic believes that wishing makes it so and his wishes are paramount because he has risen to the position of highest power. He has the authority of god and morality. What he says goes. Reality be damned.

Which brings us to the President's Achilles Heel.

For those who don't know what an Achilles Heel is, it is a weakness that brings ultimate defeat. In Greek Mythology, the hero Achilles, who was half-man and half-god, was thought to have been indestructible except for his one weakness which was his heel. In the Greek poem, the Iliad, Achilles was killed by Paris who shot him with an arrow through his heel.

Regarding the President's Achilles Heel; The American people did not vote for his Health Care program, his jobs stimulus bills, his interventions, his unilateral decrees, his lawlessness. This is because most of the people are rational. They are not mere brutes who follow any lie told to them. They knew that these programs were not in their self-interest. They knew that their future hard work (in the form of debt) was merely being re-distributed; nothing was being added to the gross product...which means no "stimulation" was being accomplished. They were smarter than the President and all his professors combined.

The rationality of the American people represented the President's Achilles Heel, his deadly weakness within his perceived strength as a leader. It doesn't matter how cleverly he told a lie; it was still a lie and people could see through it.

The fantasy that you could create economic well-being by giving other peoples' money to some did not wash. You cannot indefinitely spend tomorrow's money; sooner or later you lose your credit rating and you are destitute. Wishing does not make it otherwise. Neither does fudging statistics. Numbers say one thing but the people believe what they see and experience; hunger.

The American people long ago read between the lines of the President's actions and statements. Though many of them don't know what statism is, they can see that there is something wrong with the President's manner of speaking. They ask themselves whether he was a communist, a socialist, a fascist, a welfare statist and they debate with themselves (endlessly) the meaning of what he did not say, the nature of the people that he brought into his administration, the decrees he issued, the laws he disregarded and they know that the principles he claimed to espouse, free markets and capitalism, are clearly not what he advocated.

They saw clearly that he advocated a government of men and not of laws.

You Didn't Do That

Imagine a young man who has worked hard to be a great baseball player. He is 12 years old and has spent hours doing lots of extra practice, paying rapt attention to his coaches, reading books about the lives of great baseball players such as Babe Ruth and Mickey Mantle. All of his energy is being spent in learning the sport; how to run, steal bases, hit the ball and throw it accurately. He works hard to make the All-Star Team in his local Little League and today he has hit his first home run. He is very proud of himself and can't help but express his excitement and enthusiasm to his father. On the way home from the game, he tells his father that he thinks he has a good chance of making the All-Star Team. The father explodes and tells his son:

"There are a lot of good ball players who don't think they are that good. Look, if you've hit a home run, you didn't do it on your own. You didn't get there on your own. I'm always struck by people like you who think, 'Well, it must be because I was just so smart.' Look around you; there are a lot of smart people out there. Other people hit home runs. They don't say, 'It must be because I worked harder than everybody else.' Let me tell you something — there are a whole bunch of hardworking people out there.

"If you hit a home run, somebody along the line gave you some help. There was your coach. Somebody helped create this sport for you to play. Somebody invested in ball parks and spectator stands. If you've hit a home run, you didn't do that on your own. Somebody else made that happen."

What kind of father would say this to his son? What kind of father would destroy that young man's joy and excitement by putting him down like that? Is there any justice in that statement, any appreciation for the effort and dedication that it took that young man to be able to hit the ball that far? In the face of such an attack, would that young man try harder in the future, knowing that at the end of the day, he will be ridiculed by his father for his effort? The likelihood is that if he ever hits a home run again, he will hope that his father is not there to see it.

That father has killed this young man's joy and love of accomplishment.

Now listen to this:

"There are a lot of wealthy, successful Americans who agree with me—because they want to give something back. They know they didn't—look, if you've been successful, you didn't get there on your own... If you were successful, somebody along the line gave you some help. There was a great teacher somewhere in your life. Somebody helped to create this unbelievable American system that we have that allowed you to thrive. Somebody invested in roads and bridges. If you've got a business—you didn't build that. Somebody else made that happen." — Barack Obama, C-SPAN

Hey coach, don't put me in. I've heard it before.

About Robert Villegas

Robert Villegas is an Arizona Author specializing in fiction, romance, theater and philosophy. He was born in South Texas (Weslaco) but raised in Indiana. He is Hispanic-American but American in every sense of the word. He has spent a lifetime in the business world as a UPS executive and also worked in locations all over the United States and Europe. He is an Army veteran who served in Korea as a telecommunications specialist serving in the 7th Infantry Division in Camp Casey, Korea. He was educated in Indiana and earned a Degree through the University of the State of NY (Albany) via an external degree program. He is divorced with three grown children and four grandchildren.

Alcoholism and Addiction – the System

These four books comprise a system that can be used by both patients and counselors who are battling Alcoholism and Addiction. Based upon Mr. Villegas's own system developed during his struggle against alcoholism, this system includes:

Alcoholism and Addiction – A Secular Ten-Step Program

This groundbreaking book offers a secular approach to alcoholism unlike that offered by Alcoholics Anonymous. We recommend that every individual going for alcohol and drug-abuse counseling be given a copy of this book which contains the workbook and the two versions of The World's first drunk. http://amzn.to/2md6R9w $3.45 Kindle $11.95 softcover

The Secular Ten-Step Program Workbook

This booklet covers the program developed by Mr. Villegas. It is designed as a workbook with blank spaces for the patient to write his own thoughts as he takes each of the ten steps. Order one copy for each patient in counseling. http://amzn.to/2IrHimS $4.49 Kindle $6.95 softcover

The World's First Drunk – With Counselor Talking Points

This booklet is designed for the counselor as he works with patients during individual or group therapy. It contains helpful tips on discussing the life story of the man who invented alcohol. Order one copy for each patient in counseling. http://amzn.to/2l446Wr $2.99 Kindle $5.95 softcover

The World's First Drunk – Patient Version

This version of the short story contains empty spaces where the patient can answer questions about the life story of the man who invented alcohol. Order one copy for each counselor. http://amzn.to/2ldxBGb $2.99 Kindle $5.95 softcover.

Business Books by Robert Villegas

These four books by Robert Villegas comprise some of the business books that he has written. As an executive working for several companies, he was able to develop these methods that will help anyone seeking to excel in the business world. These books are:

How to Be a Great Employee – and a Greater Manager
You cannot be a great manager without first being a great employee. And this is something that requires learning, experience and attitude. The attitude comes from you but the learning and experience you should acquire through diligent study and practice. http://amzn.to/2BqdG2i $3.99 Kindle $8.95 softcover

SWOT Analysis Supercharged
A SWOT Analysis is an objective look at the internal and external elements of your organization that impact your success or lack thereof. If done diligently, you will always have a handle on what you need to do to improve season after season.
http://amzn.to/2BCAWYx $3.99 Kindle $6.95 softcover

The Five-Module Call Center Training System
The Five-Module Call Center Training System is designed to assist the Call Center Team Leader in helping his employees quickly upgrade their skills to an acceptable level. http://amzn.to/2B3Svj1 $3.99 Kindle $5.95 softcover

Website Development Methodology
Effective strategic marketing requires the ability to differentiate the website development organization and its deliverables from those of the competition. http://amzn.to/2DnYMqh $2.99 Kindle $12.95 softcover.

   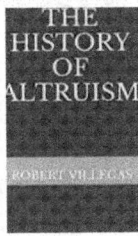

The Mark of Titus
Excerpts from the book Unkilling Jesus which highlight some of the key discoveries implied by new theories about the origin of the Jesus Myth. The idea that the Romans invented Christianity is the basic premise of new theories about the origin of Christianity
.http://amzn.to/2itMCo0 $3.49 Kindle $5.95 softcover

Contra Religion
This book is designed as a "shorter" explanation of the ideas presented in my larger book, "Behind the Ritual Mask" which seeks to define fundamental principles of religion. I'm hoping this book will serve as a primer for the original book and spur an interest in reading it. http://amzn.to/2yWMSlx $3.99 Kindle $6.95 softcover

Is this the Face that Launched a Thousand Ships?
It was love at first sight. I saw her one day while watching a television program about King Tut, whose tomb had been discovered by Howard Carter years before. I was looking at the famous bust of a beautiful Egyptian Queen. https://amzn.to/3t487x3 $3.99 Kindle $7.95 softcover

The History of Altruism
The History of Altruism is a historical treatment of the development of altruism throughout time from the Paleolithic period to today. It tracks the development of self-sacrifice of primitive man to the advent of altruism as a development from Kant's "duty". It covers a broad sweep of concepts and shows how they influenced modern man, religion and societies through the ages. https://amzn.to/3gN8zgy $4.19 Kindle 14.95 paperback.

Unkilling Jesus

Who was Paul and what was his role in the creation of Christianity? What was his provenance, and did he meet the resurrected Christ? Who wrote Revelation and what was the document's purpose? Why was Domitian assassinated?

http://amzn.to/2itMCo0 $3.99 Kindle $15.95 softcover

Domitian: The Final Messiah

The central goal of this book is to define the specific themes and concepts that make up Domitian's contribution to Christianity – in a sense, we are defining the specific Domitian overlay to the Christian materials originally developed for Titus.

http://amzn.to/2yWMSlx $2.99 Kindle $6.95 softcover

Paul's Agon and the Mystification of History

Paul and Jesus are joined in one important way; the way of a miracle. They met on the road to Damascus while Paul supposedly pursued Christians. Jesus, in a sense, told Paul to get with the program and stop persecuting his people. In this incident, the Bible tells us that Jesus is already dead, and resurrected. This book argues otherwise.

http://amzn.to/2zSDsuP $5.99 Kindle $19.95 softcover

Christianity on the Arch of Titus

This book explores the "persons" visible on the Triumphant Arch of Titus which is located in the heart of Rome. These people were significant in that they played a role, not only in Rome's conquest of Judaea but also in the creation of Christianity. This book explores those individuals and the roles they played in the creation of one of the most important religious movements in world history.

https://amzn.to/3xz3OgM $3.69 Kindle 10.95 paperback.

The REAL Purpose-Driven Life

After centuries of being told that it is not about you, it is time to set the record straight. You are a unique individual and your goal in life should be to achieve your own happiness.
https://amzn.to/2XyrpPf $3.50 Kindle $7.95 softcover

Values and Purpose Workbook

This book is about you. It's about time. After centuries of being told that nothing is about you, it is time to set the record straight. You are a unique individual and your goal in life should be to achieve your happiness. https://amzn.to/2XwlkTv $3.99 Kindle $8.95 softcover

The Real Purpose-Driven Life

After centuries of being told that it is not about you, it is time to set the record straight. You are a unique individual and your goal in life should be to achieve your own happiness. This book is about helping you accomplish your goals and fixing your purpose firmly in place. It covers not only why you should pursue your goals but how to do it.

https://amzn.to/3ebkhjr $3.99 Kindle $6.95 softcover

The Values and Purpose Workbook

Rather than give you tasks that involve doing a lot of things for other people, I'm am going to tell you that focusing on yourself will reveal your life's purpose and express your passions and freedom. I'm going to start with you.

https://amzn.to/3eQf4wG $2.99 Kindle $6.95 softcover

This Book is About You

Some people move briskly bent on a purpose, concerned only about what they are about. Some people walk by them; and do not even notice. They just keep to their path. This book is about you. It's about time. https://amzn.to/3vFMzss $2.99 Kindle $5.95 softcover

Revelation

These three books are based upon a new perspective on the document named Revelation. Based upon a new theory of the story of Jesus as an invention of the Roman Imperial Cult, these books add significant new evidence for this theory.

Coded Messages in the Pastorals
The first book in the series on Revelation. I see Christianity, as we know it today, as an outgrowth of mostly one mind and one perspective and that is the mind and perspective of Paul the apostle who was the alter-ego for another man who lived and wrote in the AD 80s and AD 90s. https://amzn.to/3xx2Gdm $4.69 Kindle $10.95 softcover

The Seven Letters of Revelation
The second book on the three-book series on Revelation. The idea that Domitian was the author, through John, of Revelation is a relatively new idea. But, if this is true, it answers many questions about the purpose of Revelation and what events led up to it. By connecting the document to Domitian, we are also able to connect it to Pauline Christianity and understand the context for both Christian writings and Revelation. https://amzn.to/3aLekb4 $3.99 Kindle $6.95 softcover

Understanding the Book of Revelation
The third in the three-book series on Revelation, Understanding the Book of Revelation is the third and final book in the series about the conflict between Paul and Domitian over Paul's version of Christianity which is found in the gospels. https://amzn.to/3tWn6dH $5.19 Kindle $8.95 softcover

Existence a Rational Thoughtbook

A Rational Thoughtbook is designed for thinking as opposed to reading. It combines brief prescient content with stunning imagery. Existence focuses on the nature of existence and gives you intelligent thoughts to integrate into your life.

https://amzn.to/2RZpsKV $4.99 Kindle $12.95 softcover

The Virtue of Independence

One of the most important goals for any person is to establish intellectual independence. Intellectual independence is the road to "life" independence, which is the ability to earn your own way without help from others. https://amzn.to/3awuCV2 $2.99 Kindle $6.95 softcover

Rational Meditation

Rational Meditation is self-meditation. It is thinking about yourself without guilt and without the tenets of modern philosophy (that the world is unknowable, that man is a phony, that ethics and living are only about others). https://amzn.to/3gus9OE $6.99 Kindle $12.95 softcover

History of My Mind

This booklet is the companion to my book entitled Rational Meditation. It utilizes the various exercises of the original book that involve contemplation or meditation and provide space for written input by the reader. https://amzn.to/3gy3hpl $4.69 Kindle $11.95 softcover.

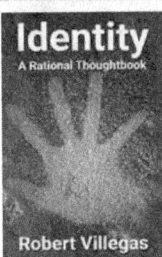

Fiction and Creative Poems and Plays

  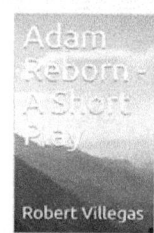 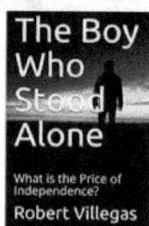

Poetic Prose and Poetry

These expressions represent some of Mr. Villegas' deepest thoughts as he lived and traveled throughout the world in locations such as Germany (East and West), Austria, Britain, Spain, Canada, France, Luxembourg, Belgium, the Netherlands, Korea, New York, Miami, San Francisco and other locations. https://amzn.to/3vu7X3B $2.99 Kindle $6.95 softcover

The Lost Poems

These poems were discovered among Mr. Villegas's archives in 2016. Many of them have been read by only Mr. Villegas. Most of these poems were rejected as "not that good". After seeing them again, he has changed his mind. These poems expressive, fresh and spontaneously honest. https://amzn.to/3aPg5nB $3.99 Kindle $6.95 softcover

Adam Reborn – A Short Play

Adam Reborn is a play of symbols. Adam and Eve, as I have portrayed them, are young and heroic people learning to deal with a Paradise and God that are hostile to them. There is no chance of life for them. https://amzn.to/3u9Nr8b $2.99 Kindle $6.95 softcover

The Boy Who Stood Alone

Jonny Payne has just discovered Ayn Rand and his parents don't know what to do. They take him to a priest and a psychologist but his only question is "What is the price of independence? https://amzn.to/3nCG6ve $3.99 Kindle $6.95 paperback.

Fiction and Creative Materials

Aphrodite
Johnny is a Spanish guitar player with a mysterious past. At a party, he meets the beautiful songstress Aphrodite who is enthralled with his flamenco guitar skills. Later, she learns they have a connection, a particular song they both appear to know. Aphrodite discovers the connection, and through dreams, the two fall in love. The question is whether they will ever be together. https://amzn.to/3xIImXZ $3.99 Kindle $5.95 softcover

The Odyssey of Amerigo the Founder
Amerigo was born in a time of desperation and dystopia. He was the only man with the vision of a great future. Many repaired to his cause while others swore to destroy him. They wanted his life, his mind and everything he loved. He swore that no matter what they did, he would win the struggle for freedom and a new future.
https://amzn.to/2Qz8h2t $3.99 Kindle $8.95 softcover

Bob and Bobbie
1967 - a town outside Camp Casey, Korea - two young people have come together to challenge a world that makes love impossible.
https://amzn.to/3sZWSpf $2.99 Kindle $5.95 softcover

The Raven Haired Girl
Bobby met Angie 52 years ago in a poor neighborhood in Indianapolis. It was love at first sight. For a few short months, their relationship blossomed into love. They were in love but didn't know how to be in love because they were only fourteen years old.
https://amzn.to/3306plF $2.99 Kindle $6.95 paperback.

Naming Names in the NT

"Discovery consists of seeing what everybody has seen and thinking what nobody has thought." - Albert Szent-Gyogyi – 1937 Nobel Laureate
https://amzn.to/3mXR66H $3.99 Kindle $9.95 softcover $16.95 hardcover

Finding Your Soft Cry

Every individual has a yearning to know that he is both free and good. This yearning comes to him from early youth, and he hopes that he eventually develops the intellectual tools to help him distinguish between his nature and the demands of society. The key to freedom is the ability to act without restriction and, especially, without guilt. https://amzn.to/3p8lY7m $3.99 Kindle $8.95 softcover $15.95 hardcover

The New Totalitarianism – Quo Vadis?

The previous century was one of the bloodiest in history. Two World Wars and many other wars do not bode well for our century that is beginning to rival the previous in its bloodlust. If we look carefully, we find in the last century the philosophical roots of the present century. The philosophers of the last century are the philosophers of the present. https://amzn.to/3AMZNFC $5.99 Kinde $10.95 softcover $25.95 hard cover

A Call to Reason

Is it possible that the problems in the world are not caused by capitalism and rich people? Is it possible that anti-capitalism and anti-reason philosophies are nothing more than elaborate hoaxes designed to convince people to give up everything they have honestly earned and take it away from them? Is it possible they are caused by the re-distribution of capital to wasteful uses and the consequent destruction of jobs and affluence? https://amzn.to/3mVNrq5 $5.99 Kindle $9.95 softcover $24.95 Hardcover

Poems for the Stage

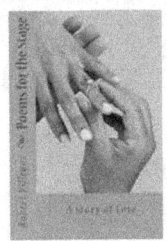 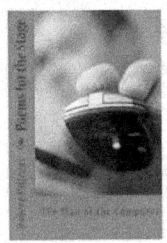

Poems for the Stage – A Story of Love

This dramatic presentation features poems found in Mr. Villegas's book Poetic Prose and Poetry. Some are also found in his book.

https://amzn.to/3gSJctV $2.99 Kindle $5.95 softcover

Poems for the Stage – The Man at the Computer

This dramatic presentation is based upon poems from Mr. Villegas's book Poetic Prose and Poetry. Some of the poems have been slightly altered to reflect the internal story. Mr. Villegas's book Poetic Prose and Poetry can be found on Amazon.com.

https://amzn.to/2R8zpFf $2.99 Kindle $5.95 softcover

A Boomer takes on the Far Left

I just learned something about myself – and it isn't very good. In fact, it is very bad. I learned that the opinions of Boomers don't matter any more. We are obsolete in this new age of new knowledge. Anything we think is unimportant and false. I don't think so. https://amzn.to/3tzNqtc $5.19 Kindle $10.95 softcover

Crushing the Alinsky Radicals

The worst enemy of individual rights today is a group of people I call the Alinsky Radicals. These people are now in charge of our culture and temporarily, in charge of government. They are associated, philosophically and politically, with the communists and fascists of the past. They are not your father's liberals. They are the direct descendants of dictators such as Stalin and Mao. In this book, I hope to convince you of the evil of the Alinsky Radicals and to provide the intellectual ammunition you need to eradicate them from society. https://amzn.to/3hbh9WN $3.49 Kindle $8.95 softcover

The Conservative's Dilemma

I wrote this book to ask some important questions about the conservative philosophy of altruism. https://amzn.to/3bfDQ8e $2.99 Kinde $6.95 softcover.

The Biggest Mistakes in History – 2008 to 2016

To be the Chief Executive of the greatest country in the world requires a leader with a great deal of knowledge, experience and reasoning ability. It requires having the very best minds as advisors, minds that the President can count on to give reasoned arguments and detailed knowledge about the important issues of the day. I think it takes a special ability to understand the principle of cause and effect concerning how government action impacts the lives of real people. https://amzn.to/3tDQ4Ol $2.99 Kindle $10.95 softcover

Dachau and Berlin in 1990

This booklet chronicles Mr. Villegas' thoughts during visits to Dachau and Berlin during 1990, disclosing my observations of milestones in German history, past and present, and relating those events to world happenings as they were unfolding at the time. I traveled throughout Germany for much of 1990 while on business. https://amzn.to/3ex578d $2.99 Kindle $6.95 softcover

What Harvard and Princeton Don't Want You to Know

The professors at Harvard and Princeton don't want you to know about the worst ideas in history. This is because they have been pawning these ideas off as true and profound. They have been using them to deceive and manipulate us for centuries. https://amzn.to/3farP5p $5.19 Kindle $9.95 softcover

Defending American Values

This book is made up of several chapters about American values and how they can be defended without a descent into the abyss of dictatorship. The book argues for individual rights and provides reasons why we should fight for them. https://amzn.to/3uMFq9L $3.99 Kinde $5.95 softcover.

Capitalism Doesn't Fail

How many times have we heard the old saw: "Capitalism has failed again" over the course of contemporary events? We heard it during the Great Depression of 1929 after Hoover had invoked tariffs and precipitated economic retaliation and a banking crisis. Along with this question usually came a statement to the effect, that "We can fix capitalism and make it even stronger by issuing economic controls or spending money to stimulate economic activity." https://amzn.to/3xZIAJ6 $4.19 Kindle $10.95 softcover

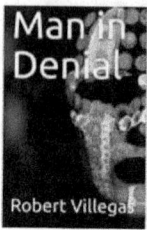 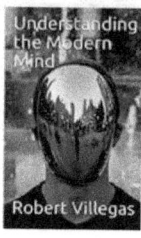  

Naming Names in the NT

If psychology has no solid epistemology and metaphysics, how can it stand on its own? I do not think it can and this explains why psychology is in such a sad state today. Yet, before we can put psychology on a solid foundation, philosophy too must advance above the level of puberty. With its base in modern philosophy, even philosophy cannot stand on its own which exposes the real problems with modern psychology. https://amzn.to/3oVTDAQ **$5.99 Kindle $9.95 softcover $18.95 hardcover**

Finding Your Soft Cry

The purpose of this book is to delve into critical issues about how the human mind has come to the modern position of doubt and despair. The culprits in this matter include the irrationality of both rationalism and skepticism, and, in particular, the child of skepticism known as pragmatism.
https://amzn.to/3mRLZF9 **$6.99 Kindle $9.60 softcover $26.95 hardcover**

The New Totalitarianism – Quo Vadis?

One of the fathers of critical theory was Herbert Marcuse who escaped European dictatorship only by coming to America. America gave him the freedom and protection he needed to destroy capitalism in America.
https://amzn.to/2YW9LaS **$4.99 Kinde $8.95 softcover**.

A Call to Reason

A logical fallacy is a faulty thought process that violates a rule of proper thinking. Correct arguments are defined as proper generalized expressions that define logical truths or knowledge. In effect, a rule of logical reasoning addresses all of the common modes of valid argument while the faulty argument contradicts them. This book examines altruism as a logical fallacy.
https://amzn.to/3vdFiB0 **$5.99 Kindle $9.95 softcover $18.95 Hardcover**

Finding Sponsors 1 and 2

This book is written for anyone seeking sponsorship relationships in the sport and entertainment fields. The ideas and principles presented here are applicable to any company, sport team, entertainment company, marketing agency and charitable organization that uses corporate sponsorships to support its activities. Volume 1: https://amzn.to/3ejm1Hp $5.19 Kindle $12.95 softcover Volume 2: https://amzn.to/3eVDo0e $4.69 Kindle $10.95 softcover

How to Write a Sponsorship Proposal

This booklet provide you with some basic guidelines on what to communicate in order to produce a winning sponsorship proposal. These guidelines will focus on what you should be presenting to your potential sponsor to make the best business case for involvement with your team or entertainment company. https://amzn.to/3tpHRxs $2.99 Kindle $6.95 softcover

Hospitality Event Planning Handbook

One key part of your sponsorship activation strategy might be customer hospitality events in conjunction with sporting events. How do you pull off a Hospitality Event for your biggest customers? You may not know how to start, what to do and how to ensure the event is a success. This book can help. http://amzn.to/2mxzpgy $7.95 softcover.

Selling Sponsorship in the Age of the Coronavirus

This book provides suggestions on how sport teams, athletes and concert promoters can mitigate the damage done to their businesses by the economic lockdowns (due to the Coronavirus). It integrates checklists, SWOT Analysis and other valuable business aids into one toolkit that will help you keep your sport and/or genre alive in these difficult times. https://amzn.to/2QVBNiM $5.15 Kindle $5.95 softcover

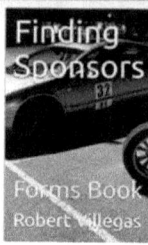   

Finding Sponsors Forms Book

This "Forms Book" is intended to provide samples of the forms mentioned in my book "Finding Sponsors for Sport and Entertainment". This will make it possible for you to reproduce these forms in other formats as well as download the forms document from the **SponsorProAZ** website for use with Microsoft Word. https://amzn.to/3b95yDW $2.99 Kindle $5.50 softcover

Submitting Your Sponsorship Proposal Online

This booklet enables sport teams and concert promoters to submit their sponsorship proposals to companies that accept only online submission of proposals. https://amzn.to/3euzdti $2.99 Kindle $5.95 softcover

The Art of Sponsorship

This short book is based upon Mr. Villegas' book "Finding Sponsors for Sport and Entertainment". It is also based upon a course that he taught for an organization managing Indiana Parks and Recreation facilities. It is, in a sense, a condensation of information from the book geared toward organizations that would like to earn revenues on their facilities through corporate sponsorship. https://amzn.to/3beuVnC $2.99 Kinde $6.95 softcover.

Restarting Your Business After the Pandemic

This new book is designed to help you restart your business after the Coronavirus pandemic. You will find here all the right questions, how you can find the answers and the forms you need to walk through your restart and coming success. https://amzn.to/2QVBNiM $5.15 Kindle $5.95 softcover